LEAD, KINDLY LIGHT

LEAD, KINDLY LIGHT

Studies of the Saints and Heroes
of the Oxford Movement

By

DESMOND LIONEL MORSE-BOYCOTT

Essay Index Reprint Series

BOOKS FOR LIBRARIES PRESS
FREEPORT, NEW YORK

First Published 1933
Reprinted 1970

STANDARD BOOK NUMBER:
8369-1529-1

LIBRARY OF CONGRESS CATALOG CARD NUMBER:
70-107728

PRINTED IN THE UNITED STATES OF AMERICA

TO

THE CHORISTERS

OF ST. MARY THE VIRGIN

SOMERS TOWN

JULY 2, 1932   THE DAY OF DEDICATION
St. Mary of the Angels   OF THEIR CHOIR SCHOOL

CONTENTS

7

LEAD, KINDLY LIGHT

I

INTRODUCTION

THE ROMANCE OF THE CENTURY

THE Keble centenary in 1933, which the whole of the Anglican Communion is about to celebrate, will be a silent comment upon the attitude of the Church in former days to the great Oxford leaders; a time for the powers that are to ask themselves whether, in building the tombs of the prophets, they are consistent in stoning their children; and for the children to ask whether they are legitimate or otherwise. A survey of a century of the Oxford Movement, better known now as Anglo-Catholicism, cannot but be profitable.

A century ago England was a land of closed churches and unstoled clergy. The Sacraments were seldom, and often irreverently, administered. The altar was a mean table, as often as not, which the parson would have been ashamed to have in his kitchen; and the verger would place his bucket and dustpan on it when he came to do the cleaning. Art

9

was weeping in the wilderness, and old churches were as disfigured as new ones were hideous. The parson was often an absentee, not infrequently a drunkard. Bishops filled their aprons with emoluments from sinecures, and did but little work. The rich went to church to doze in upholstered, curtained pews, fitted with fireplaces, while the poor were herded together on uncomfortable benches. The lynx-eyed beadle would pounce with his wand upon any child in the gallery who failed to attend to the tedious dronings of clerk, reader and parson, perched one above the other in the pagoda-like three-decker.

From the organ-loft came garish music, village singers vying to over-top one another in the metrical mutilation of the psalms by Tate and Brady. Prayers were, as Newman said, clipped, pieced, torn, shuffled about at pleasure, until the meaning of the composition perished, and what had been poetry was no longer even good prose. Where once the scent of incense had hung about the ancient walls there was, instead, the odour of snuff, and the smell of dust and damp. The Royal Arms had taken the place of the crucifix. Ugly boxes of wood frowned upon the congregation, from which the preacher moralized by the hour, and our ancient cathedrals were more like tombs than palaces of God.

Lord Halifax has told us that when he was a child the Holy Communion was celebrated in his parish church only four times a year. Lent and Holy Week were unobserved ; although, without anyone knowing why, the Shriving Bell was rung at noon on Shrove Tuesday, and a merry clamour was made each Sunday morning at 8, though no one remembered any service at that early hour.

The bells tolled of a past as dead as good Queen Anne. In obscure parts of the country, perhaps, some ancient customs lingered. A dairy-woman might fast from dawn to noon on Sacrament Sunday, as her mother had done before her, but she would be an anachronism.

The Church got the clergy she deserved, comfortable fellows who thought more of the things of earth than the things of Heaven. The weakness began from above. A bishop's chaplain examined two candidates for Holy Orders in a tent on a cricket field where he was playing. Another examined a candidate while he (the chaplain) shaved, and required him to construe two words.

Bishops were absentees from their dioceses for years. In *Mansfield Park* the summit of clerical achievement seems to be reached when the fashionable female rejoices at dinner that her clerical flame in no wise betrays his profession by his dress. Mr. Pickwick's Christmas at Dingley Dell is also informative. Of holly and mistletoe and plum-pudding and cheering drink there is abundance. The decorations are complete when a parson flits across the stage, but the revellers no more think of worshipping in the early morning than of cutting off the parson's nose. It is true that they attend the " morning service," but

the morning service was what Dickens had been
wont to find in his boyhood in the church which I
serve, St. Mary the Virgin, Somers Town, that is, a
long, dreary Mattins with a prosy sermon. None
cares more than I for the Choir Office of Mattins,
but the point of view of the Oxford leaders was that
Mr. Pickwick's Christmas had lost the meaning of its
suffix.

There was a Member of Parliament named Thomas
Massey who at least recognized the meaning of
" mas," which he regarded as stinking of Popery. He
moved that it be altered to " tide." Christmas would
be Christ-tide and Michaelmas, Michael-tide. He
was given his quietus by an opponent who called
him Mr. Tom-tide Tidey.

It is beyond argument that the Church was, broadly
speaking, spiritually moribund and discredited utterly.
Her general, if rather later, existence, is it not written
in the Books of Barchester? There were a few
earnest men who deplored her imminent collapse.
The Wesleyan Movement had seceded, for no beating
of enthusiasm could be welcomed in her bosom:
Wesleyanism might have saved the Church in the
early nineteenth century, as General Booth might
have saved her (for the poorer classes) in a later
generation. Great movements ever fare badly within
her borders, and are usually driven out. Perhaps, if
St. Francis of Assisi had been an Anglican, the bishops
would have driven him into founding a Salvation
Army. That eccentric genius, Father Ignatius, met

with the sternest opposition to his attempt to revive the Benedictine Order in the Church of England, and only ruins now remain as his memorial where there might be flourishing monasteries. The wonder is that the Oxford Movement has never been driven out. Multitudes of individuals have " gone out," but the Movement has gone on.

As a result, the Church is now a very lively body. Dean Inge, who has no sympathy whatever with Anglo-Catholicism, would be horrified were there no more than six communicants in St. Paul's on Easter Day, as in 1800. We should be distressed to read in our newspapers that a dead cat had been thrown into the Archbishop of Canterbury's carriage, as into Archbishop Howley's, in his own cathedral city, even though he were merry enough to rejoice that it was not a live cat. One would have to search far and wide before one could nowadays find a church in which the consecrated bread is thrown into the farm-yard, or the remains of the chalice are poured back into the bottle. I doubt if such things are done. But they were done frequently a century ago. In the lowest of churches things are done decently and in order. There were riots over surpliced choirs less than forty years ago ; now an unsurpliced choir is an oddity. The early Anglo-Catholics would rejoice with exceeding great joy could they but see how the wilderness has blossomed like the rose.

Newman little thought, when he rode along the country lanes on his horse, delivering parcels of his tracts at remote parsonages, that the Church's future was in the hollow of his hand. He despaired of the dry bones in the end, but what he thought in private when, full of days and honour, he wore a Cardinal's hat, none knows. It must have been a great puzzle to him to see his Movement feed upon one disaster after another, and grow more vigorous, and bring to birth the monastic and conventual life (the lack of which had been, in Père Lacordaire's eyes, the token that there was no Catholic ancestry to which the Anglican Communion could lay claim); revive the ancient glories of plainsong and Church art; and in a thousand parishes, especially in the slums, kindle lights from the dying torch that had fallen from his hand. Newman used sometimes to go into St. Paul's Cathedral to hear the boys sing, and would weep. Was that a token? But Manning became too ultramontane to regret. . . .

When John Keble preached the " Assize " Sermon in 1833 he had no notion that he was inaugurating a movement. Newman and Richard Hurrell Froude were associated with him, and Dr. Pusey came in later. The " Tracts for the Times " resulted, a fact that is interesting from a literary point of view. Tracts were very worn-out weapons to choose, for they were in ill-favour, having sunk to the "Converted Washerwoman" stage. These, which varied in length from four-page leaflets to large treatises, took England by storm. But Froude died young, and Newman " went out " in '45. A counter and

Romanizing Movement endangered the future. Its leaders, younger and less experienced and sober, " Ideal " Ward (who saw in Rome the pattern of the Church), Dalgairns, Oakeley, of the Margaret Street Chapel, Christie, and Faber (who wrote " Hark ! hark, my soul," and many hymns now sung by all Communions) went out, too. Herein is food for thought. In the Catholic movement of to-day there are like schools, of sober High Anglicanism and extreme Anglo-Catholicism. Yet Rome gains more from the former than the latter, whereas the contrary was the case in early days.

Archdeacon Manning, of Lavington, near Chichester, went in '51, to become a Cardinal, to stand for a glittering moment (it is said) on the steps of the Papal Throne, from which, in magnificent renunciation, he turned away. Canon Ollard has said of him : " Memories of ' the Archdeacon,' as they called him, still survived among the older folk at Lavington in the present century. The shepherds and downsmen remembered the sound of the bell ringing for the daily office, and the figure of a tall man with a cloak over his surplice who passed them twice daily on his way to church." They were then little boys, gathering mushrooms on the dew-drenched downs at dawn.

The Movement survived by a miracle. It ceased to be mainly academic, and became parochial. While Dean Church and Canon Liddon were storming intellectual strongholds, lights were kindled in the

slums which no persecution could quench.
Mackonochie, who died in the Scottish snows,
guarded by two faithful dogs, sleeping like a tired
child after stressful years at St. Alban's, Holborn;
Father Stanton, tenderest teacher and golden preacher,
a true Father O'Flynn; Dolling in Portsmouth, a
rollicking Irishman with a passion for souls; the
Pollock brothers, of Birmingham; Arthur Wagner,
who founded one Catholic centre after another in
Brighton; John Mason Neale, first hymnologist in
Europe, and a host of others were translating into
parochial action the donnish Oxford Movement.
The conventual and monastic life began to grow
up. Dr. Pusey established the first sisterhood,
and the strange, wilful, meteoric Father Ignatius
sought, as I have said, to accustom the mind
of the Protestant Englishman to the notion of
monasticism, while Father Benson laid a sure
foundation at Cowley.

Eminent Anglo-Catholics are now to be found
in every walk of life, notable for their cheeriness
and liberal outlook, as if they are determined to
laugh themselves through the great adventure of
restoration. One seldom finds the austere, other-
worldly spirit of the Tractarians, but no doubt
each dispensation must reveal unity in diversity.

The Movement has suffered many losses, especially in the field of literature. Robert Hugh Benson,
that doughty apologist G.K.C., Ronald Knox (never
so brilliant as when writing impish essays for the

Anglican Society of SS. Peter and Paul, in the days when it offered its wares half-price to bishops and deans, while the C. of E. rocked in merriment or writhed in wrath ; as the case was), have gone. So, too, that devoted missionary priest and writer of spiritual treatises, Robert Keable, better known to the general public as the author of a dreadful book called *Simon, called Peter*, and Miss Sheila Kaye-Smith, whose *End of the House of Alard* seemed to herald the coming in our midst, at last, of a first-rate Anglo-Catholic novelist. And Father Vernon's secession shook many souls, and was again a warning to the bishops (who had been proud, in some cases, to point to him as an example of non-extreme Catholicism) that Rome often wins the moderate, while the " extremist " remains unshaken.

On the stage there is Sybil Thorndike, a splendid representative of Anglo-Catholicism. In public life there are Lord Lloyd, Mr. George Lansbury and Sir Samuel Hoare, and it should not be forgotten that Lord Irwin, the former Viceroy of India, is the son of the " Lay Pope " of the Anglican Communion, Viscount Halifax, who inaugurated the Malines Conversations.

Of clerics there are, of course, legions, and it is computed that nearly a quarter of the Anglican clergy are definite Anglo-Catholics, while many more are under the influence of the Movement. Of these it must suffice to notice such astonishing figures as Maurice Child (a modern John Inglesant),

Wilfrid Knox (known as " Rags and Tatters," a quiet but brilliant brother of "Evoe" of *Punch* and Father Ronald Knox) ; "Nippy" Williams, of Oxford, who has achieved a first-rate reputation by his effort to synthesize Anglo-Catholicism with modern science ; Prebendary Mackay, of All Saints', Margaret Street, feared by bishops and able to influence them, and train them (at least three of his clergy have become bishops) ; monks as diverse as Father Waggett, of Cowley (who is alleged to have said, satirically, perhaps even seriously, that "the bishops would be all right if they would leave religion alone "), and the monk-bishop of Truro ; and elderly, venerable scholars such as Dr. Darwell Stone, a modern Thomas Aquinas, who would go to the stake for a comma. I could quote names indefinitely. Of saints there are legion, and the memory of Father Wainwright dying in his garret in the London Docks is a reminder that although the monasteries and convents are making lovely lives, the plain parish priest, beset by the difficulties incidental to parochial life, is also enhancing the Church's glory.

But the hero of the Movement is still Frank Weston, the late Bishop of Zanzibar, a man in a million, nay more, of a century, even of an æon. When the mourning bells tolled in the cathedral of Zanzibar, built where the old slave market that inflamed the zeal of Livingstone once stood, the Anglo-Catholic Movement was moved as never before.

It is obvious that it cannot be ignored. If its

giants are not outstanding now as in days gone by it
is because the general measure of the stature of all
is higher. It is unparalleled in history. It is a
potent force in slums, in the countryside, and in
genteel circles. It occupies vast tracts of the mission
field. Yet I would say that its glory lies not primarily
in its wide appeal, but in its capacity to " stay put,"
come what come may, proscribed, persecuted,
despised and misunderstood, and unpopular with
the people.

Its need at the moment is for wise leadership, and
that is hard to come by. Perhaps no leader comes
because the moment is not ripe for a cut-and-dried
policy, because its vocation is to permeate the whole
Church rather than stride off in one direction. But
in time to come the problem of *authority* must be
settled. In the early days the battle was over the
fundamental question of whether the Anglican Church
was a new one made at the Reformation, or the old
one in spite of the breach with Rome. To a large
extent that battle has been won. There are few well-
educated critics who would dare to say that she is
merely a Protestant body, born at the Reformation,
like Merlin offspring of a spryte and a nun—a new
version of Christianity, a sect that has cornered the
Faith. Her claim to be Catholic in creed and character has been vindicated. Yet the Church of
Augustine was not originally independent of the rest
of Catholic Christendom, and cannot remain so.
The movement towards inter-Communion with the

Orthodox Churches of the East and the Old Catholics revives our longing for corporate re-union with the Latin Church. But as yet our bishops are concerned with lesser questions, even while the saints before the altar cry " How long ? "

The Anglo-Catholic Movement is both the spur and the whip, and the very power of activity, too. It lives, to vary the metaphor, to dig again the choked-up wells. It speaks the voice of the Universal Church up to the moment when she broke asunder in the ninth century, before, unfortunately, she had thought out a consistent theory of her being. And if it be urged that Anglo-Catholic teaching and practice is false, then must the Church of God have erred for nigh half her history, which, from the point of view of Churchmen, is a manifest absurdity.

Securus judicat orbis terrarum.

II

JOHN HENRY NEWMAN
1801–1890

JOHN HENRY NEWMAN is by common consent
one of the greatest figures of the nineteenth century.
" Two writers," says the historian Froude, " have
affected powerfully the present generation of English-
men : Newman is one, Thomas Carlyle is the other."

The bracketing may have been correct when Froude
was writing, and there is much to engage our interest
in Carlyle—his heroism when the manuscript of his
French Revolution, lent to a friend, was accidentally
destroyed ; his marriage with the woman whom
Edward Irving loved ; and his taciturn reaction
to life and religion ; yet he is not now one who
matters, and Newman is. His literary works can
have affected but a tithe of the persons whom
Newman's have converted to a new conception of life.
Wherever prayer is offered the sorrowful loveliness of
" Lead, kindly Light " is breathed to Heaven. The
Dream of Gerontius, from which is taken the splendid
hymn " Praise to the Holiest in the height," is, whether
considered as simple poetry, or as a musical epic when
set to Elgar, or as a precious theological treatise (and it

is really the best extant exposition of what the Christian believes to happen after death), sublime. Newman's self-depreciation was never more evident than in the circumstances of the publication of the Dream. He had thrown the manuscript into a waste-paper basket, deeming it worthless, and a friend retrieved it by chance. As for his *Apologia*, which I shall presently describe, has it not a place in the archives of imperishable things as the record written in peerless prose of a unique personality and a unique religious movement ?

John Henry Newman, the son of a London banker, was born in 1801. He was French on his mother's side, and the early religious influences which formed him were Calvinistic. He says of his childhood : " I thought life might be a dream, or I an angel, and all the world a deception, my fellow-angels by a playful device concealing themselves from me and deceiving me with the semblance of a material world."

When he went up to Trinity College, Oxford, in 1817, he was deeply religious. It is unnecessary to dwell upon his collegiate life, which was marred by ill-health, for the story really begins in 1826 when, having won in open competition a Fellowship at Oriel, he came in touch with Richard Hurrell Froude, the " Byron " of the Oxford Movement, and through him with the other early Tractarians. When Froude's ill-health necessitated a cruise abroad, Newman went with him. The cruise was singularly eventful. Not only did Newman come in contact with Roman

Catholicism (from which he reacted), but he began to see the need of the Anglican Church for an enthusiastic movement which should awaken it to vanished glories. Although optimistic, and full of youthful fire, and eagerly anxious to return to cause a stir, he was subject, also, to moods of poignant sadness. In one of these, accentuated by loneliness, while the orange-boat in which he journeyed lay in the Strait of Bonifacio, he composed what has been called the marching song of the Movement, " Lead, kindly Light."

At this point in my short review, I must leap over many years, and I think justifiably, to record an episode which has been given no place, as far as I am aware, in any of the many books on Newman, certainly not in Wilfrid Ward's ; an episode upon which I lighted by chance. If it should seem of little importance it has the merit of being new, and will interest all lovers of " Lead, kindly Light."

After Newman had become a Roman Catholic, the Rev. Edward Henry Bickersteth, some time vicar of Christchurch, Hampstead, and Bishop of Exeter, who composed " Peace, perfect peace," ventured, as Editor of the " Hymnal Companion," to improve on Newman's hymn by adding a fourth verse. It ran :

> Meantime along the narrow rugged path,
>> Thyself hast trod,
> Lead, Saviour, lead me home in childlike faith,
>> Home to my God.
> In the calm light of everlasting life,
> To rest for ever after earthly strife.

LEAD, KINDLY LIGHT

This verse, to be found in early copies of the " Hymnal Companion," was ultimately expunged, no doubt as a result of the publishers receiving the following letter by Newman, the original of which I found some years ago in an album of literary treasure trove.

GENTLEMEN,—

I doubt not I gave leave for my lines " Lead, kindly Light" to be inserted into your collection of hymns— and did so readily—but a stranger has been kind enough to inform me that your compiler has added a verse to it not mine. It is not that the verse is not both in sentiment and language graceful and good, but I think you will at once see how unwilling an author must be to subject himself to the inconvenience of that being ascribed to him which is not his own.

I have not seen it myself in the " Hymnal Companion," but the stanza has been quoted to me. It begins " Meanwhile, along the narrow, etc."

I beg you to pardon me, if this letter is grounded in any mistake.

I am, Gentlemen,
Your faithful servant,
JOHN H. NEWMAN.

If the pirate verse is beautiful, so is the remonstrance.

In 1828 Newman was appointed vicar of the University Church of St. Mary's, and there, week by week, preached those sermons, in short musical sentences spaced by long pauses, without which, according to Dean Church, " the Movement might never have gone on, certainly would never have been what it was."

Who [wrote Matthew Arnold, a vigorous opponent of the Movement] could resist the charm of that spiritual apparition, gliding in the dim afternoon light along the aisles of St. Mary's, rising into the pulpit, and then in the most entrancing of voices breaking the silence with words and thoughts which were a religious music— subtle, sweet, mournful? Happy the man who in the susceptible season of youth hears such voices. They are a possession to him for ever.

But the printed word as well as the spoken was part of the campaign, a far more important part, as events proved. To Newman we owe the inauguration of the *Tracts for the Times* which gained the name " Tractarian " for the Movement. He wrote the first, a four-page leaflet, published at a penny. The medium of the Tract seemed, then, a poor thing to use, as it had been made ridiculous by " the Converted Washerwoman " pabulum for sinners. But the tracts that no doubt fell into Mrs. Jellyby's soup *en route* for Borrioboolagha were the ridiculous, and Newman's the sublime. Newman's were for clergy ignorant of the divine principles upon which their faith was grounded, and " the Converted Washerwoman " stories were for sinners, or mere natives, with this difference, that his converted minds and hearts, while those made their recipients feel ridiculous and their distributors exalted. Within a year forty-seven tracts had been published, most of them written by Newman, and they had taken the Church by storm.

Newman would ride from village to village during the vacation, leaving parcels of them at country parsonages. Dean Church says :

> The ring of these early tracts was something very different from anything of the kind yet known in England. They were clear, brief, stern appeals to conscience and reason . . . they were like the short, sharp, rapid utterances of men in pain and danger and pressing emergency. They ceased with the publication and condemnation of Newman's Tract XC.

An interesting pamphlet on Newman, recently published, provides me with a useful paragraph which I beg leave to quote. It says :

> So far as Newman's connexion with it is concerned, the Oxford Movement falls into three distinct periods. First, the period of preparation from 1826–1833, which was marked by the ever-growing intimacy between Keble, Froude, and Newman. Second, the period of prosperity, from 1833–1841, in which, with the pulpit of St. Mary's, the Tracts, and the *British Critic* (a quarterly Review of which in 1838 he became Editor) as his organs, Newman led his gathering party from triumph to triumph. Third, the period of disillusionment and disastrous collapse, beginning with the publication of Tract XC in 1841, and ending with Newman's secession in 1845.

That secession served as a date for many a long day, and seemed to be the end of the Movement. " He went out with Newman in '45," one would say of another. If many had feared that the day of woe would come, none was ready for it. No plans were made to meet it. It simply broke hearts, none more tender than the gentle Marriott's. Newman had for some time withdrawn himself somewhat from life in Oxford by founding a sort of monastic establishment at Littlemore. His belief in the security of his controversial status was great, and he was not behindhand in trying to check and control a Romeward movement which, to use his own words, " cut into the original Movement at an angle, fell across its line of thought, and then set about turning that line into its own direction."

The dark night of his soul as an Anglican can best be told only in his own words, from the *Apologia.* He says :

The Long Vacation of 1839 began early. There had been a great many visitors to Oxford . . . and Dr. Pusey and myself had attracted attention, more, I think, than any former year. I had put away from me the controversy with Rome for more than two years. In my *Parochial Sermons* the subject had never been introduced : there had been nothing for two years, either in my *Tracts,* or in the *British Critic*, of a polemical character. . . . About the middle of June I began to study and master the history of the Monophysites. I was absorbed in the doctrinal question. This was from about June 13th to August 30th. It was during this course of reading that, for the first time, a doubt came upon me of the tenableness of Anglicanism. I recollect, on the 30th of July, mentioning to a friend, whom I had accidentally met, how remarkable the history was ; but by the end of August I was seriously alarmed. . . . My stronghold was Antiquity ; now here, in the middle of the fifth century, I found, as it seemed to me, Christendom of the sixteenth and the nineteenth centuries reflected. The Church of the *Via Media* was in the position of the Oriental communion; Rome was, where she now is; and the Protestants were the Eutychians.

He then quotes words of his own, written elsewhere, of exquisite beauty.

. . . The drama of religion, and the combat of truth and error, were ever one and the same. The principles and proceedings of the Church now were those of the Church then; the principles and proceedings of heretics then were those of Protestants now. I found it so—almost fearfully; there was an awful similitude, more awful, because so silent and unimpassioned, between the dead records of the past and the feverish chronicle of the present. The shadow of the fifth century was on the sixteenth. It was like a spirit rising from the troubled waters of the old world with the shape and lineaments of the new. The Church then, as now, might be called peremptory and stern, resolute, overbearing, and relentless; and heretics were shifting, changeable, reserved, and deceitful, ever courting civil power, and never agreeing together, except by its aid; and the civil power was ever aiming at comprehensions, trying to put the invisible out of view, and substituting expediency for faith. What was the use of continuing the controversy, or defending my position if, after all, I was forging arguments for Arius or Eutyches, and turning devil's advocate against the much enduring Athanasius and the majestic Leo? Be my soul with the Saints! and shall I lift up my hand against them? Sooner may my right hand forget her cunning, and wither outright, as his who once stretched it out against a prophet of God! anathema to a whole crowd of Cranmers, Ridleys, Latimers, and Jewels! Perish the names of Bramhall, Ussher, Taylor, Stillingfleet, and Barrow from the face of the earth, ere I should do aught but fall at their feet in love and worship, whose image was continually before my eyes, and whose musical words were ever in my ears and on my tongue!

Misgiving deepened. No kindly light cast even a retreating ray to illumine the encircling gloom of the eventide of his Anglicanism. To make matters worse for him the words of St. Augustine, "Securus judicat orbis terrarum," struck him with a power that he had never felt before. He says that they rang in his ears like "Turn again Whittington" or the "Tolle lege" of the child who converted St. Augustine himself. He was on his death-bed as an Anglican, and his passing was an agony, to himself and those who trusted and loved him, lasting many days, even unto the calamitous '45. Then the curtain fell, and the tired child tore himself away from the Church on whose bosom he had been suckled, as if she were dry and barren in dotage, to be folded in the embrace of another who never loved the child of her adopting, and wasted his talents, and disregarded his prescience of events whose shadows he alone discerned, and tricked him at length in the purple baubles of dignity; whose real reward is the love of those who come after him in the mighty army which, before his anguished eyes, had been dry bones.

How Newman wrote the *Apologia* is a story that I have written elsewhere, and, if I quote my own words, it is because no writer can easily cast the same tale into different modes of expression. Newman's secession from the Church of England had made him profoundly unpopular. He had retreated into unenviable obscurity. There seemed no " second spring " before him. If he was doing a fine work in England for the Latin Church it was in spite of frustration. Manning distrusted him. The old Roman Catholics distrusted him. His sensitive soul often writhed under Protestant gibes.

But in the beginning of 1864 he found himself put upon the defensive. He had long been aware of a vague impression to his disadvantage in the minds of the English people. It was not, perhaps, defined, but tended to portray him as one whose word could not *quite* be trusted. So long as this impression was vague, he accepted the slur in silence, as part of the cost which must needs be paid by one who, having held a dazzling and dominant position in a great movement, found himself bound to attack that which he had largely created. Charles Kingsley gave him the opportunity of winning the hearts of the people of England, and of meeting them once more upon their hearths. In a magazine article published in January, 1864, upon the theme of Queen Elizabeth, Kingsley formally and explicitly accused Newman by name of thinking lightly of truthfulness. He wrote :

Truth, for its own sake, had never been a virtue with the Roman clergy. Father Newman informs us that it need not, and on the whole, ought not to be ; that cunning is the weapon which Heaven has given to the Saints wherewith to withstand the brute male force of the wicked world. . . . Whether his notion be doctrinally correct or not, it is at least historically so.

JOHN HENRY NEWMAN

I have little sympathy with Kingsley, in spite of the fact that he wrote *The Water Babies* and played cricket with the village folk on Sundays, but I must confess, here, that I think his was a reasonable inference from the theory of "Reserve in imparting religious knowledge" favoured by Newman and other early Tractarians. There was much to be said for Reserve. They could not suddenly, in a barren and dry land, "spring" Catholic doctrines upon bigoted Protestants, even though they verily believed those doctrines to be implicit, and often explicit, in Anglican formularies. The Economical mode of teaching and arguing was necessary if they were to do their work at all. It is necessary a century later. But perhaps the definition of Economy was injudicious. Newman wrote contrasting the *Disciplina Arcani* with Economy that "the one may be considered as withholding the truth, and the other as setting it out to advantage," and would seem to have favoured the advice of St. Clement of Alexandria which I, personally, abhor.

The Alexandrian Father [he affirms] . . . accurately describes the rules which should guide the Christian in speaking and writing economically. "Being fully persuaded of the omnipresence of God," says Clement, "and ashamed to come short of the truth, he is satisfied with the approval of God, and of his own conscience. Whatever is in his mind is also on his tongue ; towards those who are fit recipients, both in speaking and living, he harmonizes his profession with his thoughts. He both thinks and speaks the truth ; except when careful treatment is necessary, and then as a physician for the good of his patients, he will lie, or rather utter a lie, as the Sophists say. . . . Nothing, however, but his neighbour's good will lead him to do this. He gives himself up for the Church." . . . . .

Such a passage as this could not but breed suspicion, and Protestants must not be blamed for assuming that to be done which was only spoken of theoretically. Kingsley should certainly be acquitted of malice, therefore, for his attack upon Newman, who seized it as a Heaven-sent opportunity of vindicating himself in the eyes of his countrymen. He answered the charge completely. He answered it unanswerably. Men might differ, thereafter, upon the rights and wrongs of the ecclesiastical disputes out of which this charge was born ; but none in his senses could doubt the integrity of John Henry Newman. A point that was readily appreciated was the fact that he had maintained unbroken silence for twenty years.

If Kingsley could not see straight when fighting Rome, because of his historical squint, he was an honest fighter, and Newman entertained the kindliest feelings towards him throughout the controversy. Kingsley keenly felt a subtlety in whatever Newman said or wrote which made his words look right, in any circumstances. Father Stanton distrusted him for a like reason. Let us forgive him for seeking behind Newman's words an intention, which was not there, and a reservation which Newman was not mentally making. Let us forgive him for losing trust in Newman, if only because he was the anvil on which the *Apologia* was hammered out.

Wilfrid Ward, in his *Life of Cardinal Newman*, says that at the close of the controversy one, and only one, adverse criticism remained permanently in the public mind—that Newman had been unduly sensitive and personally bitter towards Kingsley. But this was not so. When he heard of Kingsley's death he was deeply shocked and promptly said a Mass for the repose of his soul.

Newman's struggle to produce the *Apologia* is an epic story. He girded himself immediately to battle. Hour after hour, day after day, from dawn until midnight, for six short, but for him eternal, weeks, he sat at the desk in his untidy chamber at the Edgbaston Oratory, and penned, with aching hands, a larger work than that which the *Apologia* now is, ceasing only to pray and eat. Every other task was set on one side. His publisher, in the manner of publishers as touching relentlessness, but different, I am glad to say, in method, waited upon him for weekly instalments, accepting excuses as unreadily as Pharaoh accepted those of the Israelites when their tale of bricks was diminished and their tale of woe more bitter. Everything depended upon the *immediate* publication of Newman's own version of events, and he was work-weary and over-strung. He wept copiously throughout the time, and his manuscript was often blotted by tears.

At length it was published. Everyone read it.

Everyone changed mind. Kingsley made no reply, though he must have read with heart-searching the weekly portions as they fell from the aching hand of the Cardinal, through the press, into the hands of the public.

I have seen the little room in which the *Apologia* was written. It is not a tidy room. It is as Newman left it. Odds and ends hang upon the walls—broken rosaries and little pictures, which give one an impression of muddle and scrappiness. In his *Life* one reads that he could not find time, after a holiday, to unpack his bags for several weeks. I can imagine from this little room, containing a bed and a desk and an altar, that there was often a litter, amid the coming and the going. There was no litter in his mind. He had a wonderfully tidy mind, wherein he kept his knowledge well-docketted and cross-indexed. His prose is perfect. Dr. George Copeland wrote in 1870 to his brother William, who had been Newman's curate :

The writing of Newman, like that of Shakespeare, will admit of neither paraphrase nor translation ; and those who cannot read it in the true original had better not read it at all. I mean by the *true original*, not only the English language, established in these realms, but that pure and reformed branch of it, to which Newman, and nobody else, belongs.

Consider this passage for example :

Such were the thoughts concerning the " Blessed Vision of Peace," of one whose long-continued petition had been that the Most Merciful would not despise the work of His own Hands, nor leave him to himself; while yet his eyes were dim, and his breast laden, and he could but employ Reason in the things of Faith. And now, dear Reader, time is short, eternity is long. Put not from you what you have here found ; regard it not as a mere matter of present controversy ; set not out resolved to refute it, and looking about for the best way of doing so ; seduce not yourself with the imagination that it comes of disappointment, or disgust, or restlessness, or wounded feeling, or undue sensibility, or other weakness. Wrap not yourself round in the associations of years past, nor determine that to be truth which you wish to be so, nor make an idol of cherished anticipations. Time is short, eternity is long. *Nunc dimittis servum tuum Domine.* . . .

In character he was as near perfection as frail mortality can be. Mr. Shane Leslie has said of him that he was one of the sweetest English gentlemen who ever walked the earth, for whose sake many have tried to love our unlovely race. He was a prophet and more than a prophet, touching the secular world, foreseeing and farseeing, for his mind " measured the whole length and breadth and depth of human doubt without fascination and without dread," even though his conviction that the dry bones of Anglicanism could never be infused with life has been shown to be groundless.

He is both the glory and the tragedy of the Anglo-Catholic Movement, and, if I may be permitted to say so, a judgment upon nineteenth-century Romanism in this country. Had he stayed in the Anglican Church he would not, assuredly, have been offered a mitre, things being what they were (and are), but he could not conceivably have been humiliated, as he was humiliated in the Latin Church, by such definite hints of elevation to episcopacy that he kept a crozier in pathetic anticipation; and though he was made a Cardinal, I suspect that it was in spite of Cardinal Manning.

The most glorious son of *Ecclesia Anglicana*, he wept by the waters of Babylon to the end of his long exile from Heaven, with faithful courage that looked not back upon a step irrevocably taken. But may not we, who carry the torch that dropped from his numbed fingers, find a hint of his inner longings in the fact that sometimes, as it rang to Evensong, and evening shadows fell softly over weald and wold and throngèd city, he would make his way unnoticed into St. Paul's Cathedral to hear the singing boys, and was once discovered weeping piteously at the Littlemore of his long ago? He died on August 11, 1890. May your rest be peaceful, O Father, whom we venerate, and Angel faces you loved long since smile oft upon you, and sometimes upon us, your sons.

III

HUGH JAMES ROSE
1795–1838

To understand the vocation of the Rev. Hugh James Rose, one should repair to a Mr. T. Sikes, pastor of an obscure village in Northamptonshire, who, alone among his contemporaries at the close of the eighteenth century, possessed a spirit of prophecy. As he has fulfilled the Scriptural test of a true prophet, his words to a friend are worthy of remembrance :

The friend speaks thus to Dr. Pusey :

I well remember the very countenance, gesture, attitude and tone of good Mr. Sikes, and give you, as near as may be, what he said.

"I seem to think I can tell you something which you who are young may probably live to see, but which I, who shall soon be called away off the stage, shall not. Wherever I go all about the country I see amongst the clergy a number of very amiable and estimable men, many of them much in earnest, and wishing to do good. But I have observed one universal want in their teaching, the uniform suppression of one great truth. There is no account given anywhere, so far as I see, of the one Holy Catholic Church. I think that the causes of this suppression have been mainly two. The Church has been kept out of sight, partly in consequence of the civil establishment of the branch of it which is in this country, and partly out of false charity to Dissent. Now, this great truth is an article of the creed, and, if so, to teach the rest of the Creed to its exclusion must be to destroy ' the analogy or proportion of the faith ' *τὴν ἀναλογίαν τῆς πίστεως*. This cannot be done without the most serious consequences. The doctrine is of the last importance and the principles it involves of immense power, and some day, not far distant, it will judicially have its reprisals. And whereas the other articles of the Creed seem now to have thrown it into the shade, it will seem, when it is brought forward, to swallow up the rest. We now hear not a breath about the Church ; by-and-by, those who live to see it will hear of nothing else, and just in proportion perhaps to its present suppression will be its future development. Our confusion nowadays is chiefly owing to the want of it, and there will be yet more confusion attending its revival. The effects of it I even dread to contemplate, especially if it come suddenly. And woe betide those, whoever they are, who shall, in the course of Providence, have to bring it forward. It ought, especially of all others, to be matter of catechetical teaching and training. The doctrine of the Church Catholic and the privileges of Church Membership cannot be explained from pulpits ; and those who will have to explain it will hardly know where they are, or which way they are to turn themselves. They will be endlessly misunderstood and misinterpreted. There will be one great outcry of Popery from one end of the country to the other. It will be thrust upon minds unprepared and on an uncatechized Church. Some will take it up and admire it as a beautiful picture ; others will be frightened and run away and reject it ; and all will want a guidance which one hardly knows where they shall find. How the doctrine may be first thrown forward we know not, but the powers of the world may any day turn their backs upon us, and this will probably lead to those effects I have described."

"*How the doctrine may be first thrown forward we know not.* . . ." We who look back upon a century of the Catholic Revival ought to know, though we do not widely know, that Hugh James Rose threw it forward.

The elder son of a Rev. William Rose and Susanna his wife, he was born in the parsonage of Little Horsted in Sussex on June 9, 1795. His nurse, who had never had the care of a child before, seems, though very young, to have been given a free hand with him and to have used it discreetly. She taught him so well that before he could speak he could pick out letters on a chart. Before he was four he had mastered the Latin Grammar, and was an omnivorous reader. His mother says : " I recollect one summer morning (he then slept in our room)—knowing he was awake and yet not hearing him—his father asked, ' What are you doing ? ' ' Reading Knox's *Elegant Extracts*.' ' You can't understand what you are reading ? ' ' O, but I can, Papa,' and he told us what it was. He was then about four years old." A few weeks later he was immersed in *The Arabian Nights*.

From Little Horsted the family removed to Uck- field, where Mr. Rose conducted a school and ministered. Hugh was a delicate child and gave them anxiety. He was given freedom to please himself in his studies, which now included Greek and Heraldry. He showed a talent, also, for drawing.

Precocious children are not attractive, but Hugh was an exception. He had a singular loveliness of character and "the 'Commandment with promise' was written indelibly on his inmost nature." Fortunately, too, he could mix with his father's scholars, and found a happy home in holidays, as he grew older, at Sheffield Place, where he tutored Lord Sheffield's son. He went up to Trinity College, Cambridge, in 1813. There he did well, and became a figure in the Cambridge Union. "From a boy," says Burgon, who struggled eagerly to rescue Rose from the limbo of forgetfulness—he is one of those who seem born to be forgotten while lesser heroes gain the haloes—

He had been a prodigious reader, and cherished, as a very young man, a burning desire to acquaint himself with every department of polite learning. It was a thirst for knowledge, of which ordinary spirits seem scarcely to have a notion. To the writers of antiquity he chiefly devoted himself. . . .

His learning, indeed, was already profound and astonished Bishop Blomfield, who wrote, in reply to a criticism made by the youthful scholar of one of his books (and that upon a subject remote): "There are not more than five people in England who really understand or care about these things; and I am glad to perceive that you are going to be a sixth." He was unsuccessful, however, in securing a fellowship at Trinity, and gave up residence in 1818, being ordained in the following year to the curacy of Buxted. He married and settled down, as far as any could tell to a life of uneventful obscurity, dividing his attention between pupils at Maresfield (where he had removed) and parochial work. But in 1821 he was given the living of Horsham. There he did a remarkable work. His people flocked to church in large numbers and he was much beloved, a faithful dispenser of the Word and Sacraments in the simple way of the old High Churchmen. His thorn in the flesh was asthma, and when he was very low in health (in 1823) he was persuaded to go abroad.

It was the phenomenon of German Protestantism, as the system was to be seen at work in Prussia, which shocked his piety, aroused his worst fears, exercised his intellect [says Burgon]. A rationalizing school, of which the very characteristic was the absolute rejection of a Divine Revelation, dominated at that time in Prussia, and furnished (him) with materials for raising his voice in solemn warning to his countrymen, at a time when in high places the fires of faith and love were burning very low.

Meanwhile another Apostle was feeling his way through the maze of German thought, and, while recognizing with alarm the possible consequences thereof, becoming convinced that it was wholly sincere and might produce much good. This was Dr. Pusey, whose tale is told elsewhere. The result was a regrettable controversy between him and Rose which engaged much attention ; but Rose was undoubtedly right in his estimate of the effect of German thought upon the Faith, and Pusey seems, in after years, to have modified his views. These two young champions of orthodoxy were seeing the same enemy from different vantage ground; Rose desired to destroy it; Pusey to find some good in it. . . .

In 1830 Rose was presented to the living of Hadleigh in Suffolk, and promptly rebuilt the parsonage. His study must rank first among the " Rooms of the Catholic Revival." I should like to write a book on the Rooms. It would be a short book, composed of seven chapters. The first Room I am about to describe. The second I describe in my chapter on Charles Marriott. The third would be Charles Kingsley's study at Eversley, and the fourth the little cell at Edgbaston where Newman penned the *Apologia*; the fifth Keble's room at Hursley; the sixth the bare cell of Cardinal Manning at Westminster; and the seventh the garret in which Father Wainwright, the saint who carried Lowder's work at Wapping into the present generation, died a few years ago. My choice is possibly arbitrary, but the theme is of interest. At least my choice of Hadleigh cannot be disputed.

There Rose founded the *British Critic*. The aim of the *Critic* was to defend the Church. One afternoon he had been visited by a London publisher who was prepared to undertake commercial responsibility if he would consent to be Editor. He had many scruples, and his health was bad, but he consented, and his organ soon became *the* Church magazine of the period. Thus he was drawn into the centre of affairs, and began to make friendships with those whose names are familiar to this day, while his own is forgotten.

We come now to that tremendous moment when the Catholic Revival took shape through the initiative of Rose. We enter Rose's study. It is a beautiful room in the back of the house, looking towards the garden. Under one window there is a desk heaped with papers, by another a large table with a round-backed chair. The table has two drawers. Its surface, shining in the sun as it falls through the window, has a blotter, and a tidy array of writing materials. It is the plain desk of a man who means business and does it. There are none of the easy chairs that would grace the room of a modern Anglo-Catholic calling a conference of clergy at a crisis. Neither are there ash-trays or a tobacco jar. Those you might find in Kingsley's study at Eversley, but a minute research into the habits of the Tractarians is entirely negative in the matter of smoking.

The chair, I have said, is a round-backed one, made for a man who has to sit upright at his work. It is a bed of suffering. Many a time has Rose sat there the long night through, hearing the clock in the hall tick away the slow watches, choking for breath. Many a dawn has he struggled out of it, exhausted in mind and body. Many a time has he sighed a deep sigh of unutterable weariness at the sight of the

literary work that gave him no respite. Poor Rose
—capable of prodigious effort, yet hampered at every
turn. To-day he is expecting visitors. He will hide
his weariness. He will assume the aspect of an alert
scholar. If his tired mind wanders away he will look
at the crucifix in a small triptych that stands behind
his silver inkpots. He has attended to the parochial
business of the day and sits in eager expectation. He
has invited his young curate to attend the conference.
The curate enters and, mindful of his low estate, keeps
silence after he has been introduced to the visitors,
who come in one by one. Mrs. Rose met them as
they came through the entrance of the old tower
built by Archdeacon Pykenham in 1495. They
inquired after Rose's health, and she told them the
truth ; after her own, and she, worn out by her husband's malady, made a bright answer. But I must
not forget the curate. His name is R. C. Trench.
He is to become Archbishop of Dublin.

The formal greetings over, the visitors are shown
to their rooms, and return again to the study. The
Rev. the Hon. A. P. Perceval and William Palmer,
quiet, serious men, come first, and quietly talk about
ecclesiological matters, and the difficulties that are
agitating Oxford. Froude joins them with a merry
jest on his lips, and whether they like it or not the
desultory talk immediately seems more in keeping
with the Common Room at Oriel than the study of
the Editor of the *British Critic*.

" A most enjoyable fellow," thinks Rose, " but

rather flippant." He watches the face of the eager, merry speaker and sees a turn of the mouth which indicates wistful yearning for something unattained, and it fills him with sympathetic melancholy. A dashing fellow indeed, in *negligé* dress, with a large cravat and very tall collar, his hair straggling all over his forehead; a "blood" by the look of him, but then, he is Froude of Oriel, and his works have gone before him. Rose has heard, perhaps, that Froude wears a hair-shirt, and wonders if the story is true. The hour points to noon, and two more visitors are expected, John Henry Newman and John Keble. At that moment the post-boy comes, and a maid brings Rose a letter.

"That's from Newman . . ." says Froude, looking over Rose's shoulder. "Isn't he coming?" "I am afraid not," says Rose, disappointedly. "He hasn't had time to turn round. Well, Keble may be here any minute, so let us pray and begin our conference." Silence falls upon the group of men. They kneel in supplication. They seat themselves. They talk, rather aimlessly at first, of the state of Church affairs, of the secularization of the State, of the possibility of Disestablishment and Disendowment, of the oblivion into which true Church principles have fallen. But let me now employ, not my imaginings, but the words of William Palmer.

We met after breakfast for some hours each day for three days, sitting round the room. Each in succession spoke on the dangers of the Church and the remedies suggested : after which we all expressed opinions. The publication of Tracts and other works was much dwelt on, but we could not settle any details. All, I believe, felt the seriousness of this,—the first attempt to combine the preservation of great essential principles. I know I was myself impressed with the importance of what we were about, but on the whole the result was disappointing : it did not lead to the practical agreement we needed. We had to adjourn the whole matter to Oxford.

They were glad to have Newman and Keble at the second session at Oxford. Keble's absence from the first was explained by the following letter, its interesting nature prompting me to give it in full :

MY DEAR FRIEND,—

Mr. Palmer has communicated to me your kind and tempting invitation, which I heartily wish it was in my power to accept. Believe me, few schemes would be more pleasant to me, if I was in a condition to indulge in schemes at all. But my Father's great age and failing health, and the circumstance that he has no one to be with him in my absence but my sister, who is never well, make me quite a home-bird,—unless when I can get my brother or some of his family to take my place : and then I am bound to be working at Hooker, who hangs on hand sadly on account of these my engagements. Nevertheless I would put by everything and come to you, if I could persuade myself that I could be of much use in discussions such as you and our friends are meditating : but I know my own deficiency in ecclesiastical learning so well as to be quite prepared to *hear* or *read* with great profit what might pass on such an occasion, but very unequal to *suggest* or *argue* points at the time. And this is really the plain truth, and makes me tolerably sure

46

that altho' I should deeply regret missing such a visit as you offer me, *your counsels* will have no great loss.

It is beyond my scope to discuss the second session, but its connexion with that convened by Rose is obvious, and we are entitled to regard him as the progenitor of all Anglo-Catholic Congresses. Burgon says :

At Oxford therefore, on their return, the friends (with Newman and Keble) took counsel together ;—Froude . . . rendering the good cause the greatest disservice in his power by speaking of the Hadleigh Conference in a letter to a friend as " *the conspiracy* " ; which letter was soon afterwards published. Undeniable however it is that the Hadleigh Conference had given definite form and substance to the idea of *united action.* . . .

The Hadleigh Conference had taken place on July 25, 1833, eleven days after the Assize Sermon had been preached by Keble. Little did the friends who met at Hadleigh know the sorrow that was gripping the heart of their host, revealed in the following letter, written a few weeks before the Conference :

It is difficult to say how much I regret the loss of Hadleigh . . . but I have not had one day's health, and hardly one night's rest, since I came . . . I am tongue-tied and hand-tied, doing nothing in my parish, and so exhausted by sitting up at night that I can hardly read or write in the day. . . . My wife, who loves this place exceedingly, behaves like a heroine about it.

He was doomed to leave, for the hand of death was upon him. For a season he worked in London, relieved by its fogs and smoke. Then important work was thrust upon him at Durham. It soon overwhelmed him and he had to abandon it. He became the friend and confidant of Archbishop Howley, who was favourable to the Movement in its early stages ; and that may account for his perturbation later when the *Tracts for the Times* assumed a different and more extreme character. An important aspect of Rose's work was undoubtedly his influence over the Archbishop, who was of a pliable disposition, though capable of being moved on occasions, as when he declared he would rather resign than consecrate Dr. Arnold as a bishop. Indeed, his meekness was never more apparent than when he was mobbed in the streets of Canterbury.

In 1836 Rose became Principal of King's College, London, dying on December 22, 1838, at Florence, attended by his wife. He was buried in " a retired and lovely spot . . . situated just without the limits of the city of Florence, on the road to Fiesolé," which, judging by the large size of the cypress trees, had once been a garden. Some thirty years later the tomb was discovered in a neglected condition. The cypress trees were gone. Florence, like every growing city, had swallowed up the peaceful country-side. What had once been a walled enclosure on a little declivity, seemingly shut out from the world—" the dark foliage of the funereal garden contrasting grandly with the everlasting hills "—had become an eyesore in the midst of a throbbing city. Little it matters, though surely no Anglo-Catholic should go to Florence without making pilgrimage to his resting-place if it can now be found. It matters more that the Anglican Communion has well-nigh forgotten him who, to use the felicitous phrase of Newman, " when hearts were failing, bade us stir up the strength that was in us, and betake ourselves to our true Mother."

IV

RICHARD HURRELL FROUDE
1803–1836

RICHARD HURRELL FROUDE was the son of a country clergyman, and, like many sons of the clergy, a naughty boy. Born at Dartington, Devonshire, on Lady Day, 1803, he was destined to become the gadfly of the Oxford Movement. We are given a glimpse by his mother of the petulant nature that was, when dedicated to the service of God, to spur all the Oxford leaders into an activity that might have been only occasional, or even temporary, had there been no restless extremist to egg them on. Extremists are very useful for the prevention of settlement into ruts, and, as the child is father to the man, we need not be surprised by Mrs. Froude's description of her fractious eldest child. She says:

From his very birth his temper has been peculiar; pleasing, intelligent, and attaching when his mind was undisturbed, and he was in the company of people who treated him reasonably and kindly; but exceedingly impatient under vexatious circumstances; very much disposed to find his own amusement in teasing and vexing others; and almost entirely incorrigible when it was necessary to reprove him.

Probably she sighed with relief when the day came for him to go to his first school at Ottery St. Mary, where he stayed until he was thirteen. Thence he went to Eton. He was eighteen when the gentle, restraining influence of his mother was withdrawn by death, and a few weeks afterwards he came under John Keble at Oriel, whose holy life and teaching had a profound effect upon him. When Keble left Oxford in 1823, at the zenith of his fame, to minister to a handful of country folk, he took Froude, with Robert Wilberforce and Isaac Williams, to read during the Long Vacation, and this period was the turning-point in Froude's life. Isaac Williams gives us, in his *Autobiography*, a homely story of their first day at Southrop. He says :

It was a very rainy day when I travelled outside a coach from London to Lechlade, where I slept that night, and Keble came and took me to Southrop the next morning. He said, as his house was not yet furnished, and he could not receive us, he thought of our lodging at a farmhouse, called Dean Farm, a solitary place on the Cotswold. We walked over to see it, about four miles, I think, with Froude, who was also there. It was in the evening, and Keble was out when we started from Southrop. It came on a thick mist and rain, and the night was perfectly dark, and I wandered out the whole night till near the morning. The next day I was laid up, and Keble sent me a bottle of wine and other things, it being, I think, Sunday. For six weeks we stayed at this Dean Farm, riding over every day to Southrop, and at the end of that time Keble took us into his house, where I formed a most valued friendship with Froude. He was an Eton man, and at Oriel, of a little older standing than myself. There was an originality of thought and a reality about him which were very refreshing.

The friendship there begun between Froude and Williams quickly ripened at Oxford, "Keble being a great bond between us," as Williams says. We see the Oxford Movement in its nursery. Keble, the saint and poet and scholar, swaying from a distance two young disciples, one of whom (Froude) was to bring in Newman, who in turn was to bring in Pusey, by persuading him, in a casual conversation, to contribute a paper to the *Tracts for the Times*; and the other (Williams), by his Tract on *Reserve in Communicating Religious Knowledge*, to provoke an uproar in Protestant England like the explosion of a mine, a foretaste of that persecution which was to come upon Anglo-Catholics for a century, in every way conceivable, from the suspension of Pusey at Oxford to the breaking down with axes and hammers of the beauties of the church of St. Hilary, Marazion, in the year of gracelessness, 1932.

Froude became a Fellow of Oriel in 1826, with Newman as his colleague. He was shy of Newman, but as the latter was moving slowly away from Evangelicalism, and his Liberalism was becoming tempered by the Catholic view of Apostolic Succession, they soon had a common platform. "Newman is a fellow," he wrote at first, "that I like more the more I think of him; only I would give a few odd pence if he were not a heretic." At the end of his life he wrote: "Do you know the story of the murderer who had done one good thing in his life? Well; if I was ever asked what good deed I had ever done, I should say that I had brought Keble and Newman to understand each other."

Storm clouds were gathering over the Church in 1832 when Froude was obliged to go abroad for his health. His father, Archdeacon Froude, and Newman went with him. The consumption to which Froude succumbed some eight years afterwards, though a grievous chastisement, crippling his activities when they seemed most necessary to the Movement, was a blessing in disguise. It enabled Froude and Newman to think things out at a distance, to formulate a plan, albeit a vague one, and to gather strength of mind and body for the first years of stress and strain. Newman has somewhere said (the reference eludes me) that when for the first time he saw Rome in the distance he desired to take the shoes from off his feet and walk into the holy ground as used the pilgrims of old to do. He had a sense of history which fought with his abhorrence of Romanism. Froude, on the other hand, could see some good in Rome and beneath the shadow of the seven hills was inspired to create a slogan for the Movement which, with great respect, I suggest the leaders of modern Anglo-Catholicism might adapt. " It has throughout a touch of defiance, a breath of war." *You shall know the difference now that I am back again* might well become

LEAD, KINDLY LIGHT

You shall know the difference now that we are humbled by the new persecution. Froude was the embodiment of this spirit and returned to England thirsting for the fray, in advance of Newman.

He returned full of energy and of a prospect of doing something for the Church, and we walked in the Trinity College Gardens [says Isaac Williams] and discussed the subject. He said in his manner, " Isaac, we must make a row in the world. Why should we not ? Only consider what the Peculiars (i.e. the Evangelicals) have done with a few half-truths to work upon ! And with our principles, if we set resolutely to work, we can do the same." I said, " I have no doubt we can make a noise, and may get people to join us, but shall we make them really better Christians ? If they take up our principles in a hollow way as the Peculiars (this was a name Froude had given the Low Church party) have done theirs, what good shall we do ? " To this Froude said, " Church principles, forced on people's notice, must work for good. However, we must try ; and Newman and I are determined to set to work as soon as he returns, and you must join with us. We must have short tracts, and letters in the *British Magazine*, and verses, and these you can do for us—and get people to preach sermons on the Apostolical Succession and the like. And let us come and see old Palmer (i.e. the author of the *Origines Liturgicæ*) and get him to do something." We then called on Palmer, who was one of the very few in Oxford—indeed the only one at that time—who sympathized with us, and, although he did not altogether understand Froude, or our ways and views—the less so as he was not himself an Oxford but a Dublin man—yet he was extremely hearty in the cause ; looking more to external, visible union and strength than we did, for we only had at heart certain principles. We, i.e. Froude, Keble, and myself, immediately began to send some verses to the *British Magazine*, since published as the *Lyra Apostolica*.

The Oxford Movement was begun four days after Froude's return by Keble's Assize Sermon on National Apostasy, and ten days later he attended the conference in the beautiful rectory of Hadleigh in Suffolk, presided over by Hugh James Rose, its incumbent. Newman and Keble were prevented from attending, but William Palmer and the Rev. the Hon. A. P. Perceval were there. They agreed to fight for the Catholic doctrine of the Apostolic Succession, as taught in the Prayer Book, and to form a Society, if that were possible, and to prepare addresses from clergy and laity to the Archbishop. These quiet measures must have irked Froude sorely. He desired a flamboyant policy. At a council in Newman's rooms, for example, when Palmer was urging the necessity of securing the support of the " higher " clergy, Froude, stretched on Newman's sofa, interrupted with : " I don't see why we should disguise from ourselves that our object is to dictate to the Clergy of this country, and I, for one, do not want anyone else to get on the box."

He was not, however, to be allowed to play an active part, for his health necessitated another long absence abroad. " I am like the man," he said, " who fled full soon on the first of June, and bade the rest keep fighting." But though his presence was withdrawn he was weighty in letters, and contributed four of the *Tracts for the Times*. For awhile he acted as mathematical tutor at Codrington College in the Barbados, returning to England in May, 1835, and dying on February 28 of the following year, to the grief of his friends and the irreparable loss of the Movement.

And then his friends put their hands to a work which caused an astonishing commotion, and seemed to many to be a blunder. Froude's letters and journals were collected and published under the title *Remains*. The error lay in forgetfulness of the fact that the readers of the *Remains* had for the most part never met Froude; never been stimulated by his brilliant mind; never plumbed the depths of his sensitive soul. Dean Church says:

The *Remains* lent themselves admirably to the controversial process of culling choice phrases and sentences and epithets surprisingly at variance with conventional and popular estimates. Friends were pained and disturbed; foes naturally enough could not hold in their overflowing exultation at such a disclosure of the spirit of the Movement. Sermons and newspapers drew attention to Froude's extravagances with horror and disgust. . . . The friends who published Froude's *Remains* knew what he was; they knew the place and proportion of the fierce and scornful passages; they knew that they really did not go beyond the liberty and the frank speaking which most people give themselves in the *abandon* and understood exaggeration of intimate correspondence and talk. . . . They seem to have expected that the picture which they presented of their friend's transparent sincerity and singleness of aim, manifested amid so much pain and self-abasement, would have touched readers more."

He adds the comment: "But if the publication was a mistake, it was the mistake of men confident in their own straight-forwardness."

To Froude's *Remains*, to Isaac Williams's Tract on *Reserve in Communicating Religious Knowledge*, and to Newman's secession must be attributed the suspicion which has made pious Protestants hold up their hands in holy horror of the Movement even beyond the third and fourth generation; which has been expressed in repressive acts; and has packed the Bench of Bishops with demi-semi-quavering sympathizers afraid to come out in the open or purblind prelates who have bluntly persecuted. Had the early leaders been men of cunning they would have played their cards adroitly, and by peacefully penetrating the Anglican Communion have bound it in the grave-clothes of High Churchism.

Let us remember Froude with gladness; the gay cavalier of the Catholic Revival; the extremist who made men move; the *hidden* saint; the priest who prophetically urged frequent Communion (then celebrated only occasionally), the abolition of pew rents, the admission to the ministry of men of low degree, the grouping of clergy in presbyteries for the more efficient working of parishes in large cities; who attacked the system of appointing bishops, and violently opposed Establishment. Froude belongs to 1933, though were he living he would possibly find the atmosphere of Abbey House too sultry, and break its windows to let fresh air in ; the House of Mowbray too respectable, and re-found the Society of SS. Peter and Paul ; the *Church Times* closed to him, and the popular press open. He would be *news,* for his orthodoxy would be thrilling as only orthodoxy can be ; and his church would be banned by the bishop on account of Benediction, a service he would no doubt liken to the Evening Communion that bishops wink at.

But I would not end with Froude the controversialist, for Froude the saint is the finer memory. His poems, full of rugged beauty, are in the *Lyra Apostolica,* over the letter *β*. He writes :

> Lord, I have fasted, I have prayed,
> And sackcloth has my girdle been,
> To purge my soul I have essayed
> With hunger blank and vigil keen ;
> O God of mercy ! why am I
> Still haunted by the self I fly ?
>
> Sackcloth is a girdle good,
> O bind it round thee still :
> Fasting, it is Angel's food,
> And Jesus loved the night-air chill ;
> Yet think not prayer and fast were given
> To make one step 'twixt earth and Heaven.

There is the cry of one who practised what he preached. And here, in conclusion, is a token of his consciousness of the transitoriness of all things temporal : ˙

RICHARD HURRELL FROUDE
TYRE

High on the stately wall,
  The spear of Arvad hung;
Through corridor and hall
  Gemaddin's war note rung.
Where are they now? the note is o'er;
Yes, for a thousand years and more
Five fathom deep beneath the sea
Those halls have lain all silently;
Nought listing save the mermaids' song,
While rude sea monsters roam the corridors along.

Far from the wandering East
  Tubal and Javan came,
And Araby the blest,
  And Kedar, mighty name.
Now on that shore a lonely guest,
Some dripping fisherman may rest,
Watching on rock or naked stone
His dark net spread before the sun,
Unconscious of the dooming lay,
That broods o'er that dull spot, and there shall brood
        for aye.

V

ISAAC WILLIAMS
1802–1865

ISAAC WILLIAMS like Hugh James Rose and Charles Marriott is one of the overlooked heroes of the Catholic Revival, although his hymns are sung in all the churches. To write of him after Newman and Froude, is like entering a quiet bay after tossing on a tumultuous ocean; like coming upon a deep, still pool after crossing crag and torrent. Not that his hymns are suggestive of calm contentedness. " Lord, in this Thy mercy's day," beloved by Protestant and Catholic alike, strikes a note of mournful awe, and " Be Thou my Guardian and my Guide " would indicate a sorely tempted pilgrim on the highway of life rather than a quiet and gentle student.

But his hymns reflect his early character, changed, illumined and tempered by the Catholic life, to which John Keble introduced him, and softened by deep sorrows.

He was born near Aberystwith on December 12, 1802, but his early days were spent in London, where his father practised law. " We lived," he says, " at a corner of Bloomsbury Square, in a small street, where,

I believe, Newman also must have been living at the same time." He had three brothers and one sister, and lived a happy and uneventful childhood, being keen on everything that normal boys like, especially rabbits and cricket. He showed great talent in Latin, his knowledge being brought to such perfection that when he was at Oxford he could write an English essay only by first thinking it in Latin.

In his *Autobiography* (a book wellnigh forgotten, but one of the vital documents of the Movement) he frequently hints that he was affected for evil by his early companions. " Almost the first boys I came in contact with, on leaving home, produced on my mind a very startling impression. I remember then feeling, for the first time, that I understood what the Bible and the Catechism meant by speaking of the world as ' wicked.' " Of a gloomy temperament (evidently), he read and enjoyed Sherlock on *Death*, the sentences of which were to haunt his mind like strains of music.

Later, at Harrow, he was happier, and lived a freer life, his primary passion being cricket. He idled badly, though he loved Latin still. He became companionable and popular, and ran in the slippery paths of youth. He saturated himself with Byron, reading at first with a guilty conscience and then relief at finding no wickedness therein. He says : " The subtle poison of these books did me incalculable injury for many years ; the more so as the infidelity was so veiled in beautiful verse and refined sentiment." He received no religious instruction at Harrow, and looked back upon his life there with such horror that he dreaded to send his own children to school, and delayed doing so. He was flattered and tempted on every hand, and was set fair for a life of sin and scepticism when he entered Trinity College, Oxford.

This would seem to have been the most deplorable period of his young life, but Providence was planning trivial accidents. One of them was a friendship with a clergyman who knew Keble, then a tutor at Oriel, and he promised to introduce him. It was 1822. The clergyman, a Mr. Richards, who lived at Aberystwith, arranged the introduction there, when Keble came to see him, and it so happened that Isaac Williams and Keble rode some way with him through the rugged Welsh country-side. On returning to Oxford he saw nothing of Keble, however, for a year. He says : " I . . . thought he had forgotten me . . . when I succeeded in getting the Latin verse prize. . . . He then appeared in my rooms, on the ground-floor opposite the garden at Trinity, and said he had come to ask whether he could assist me in looking over my prize poem before it was printed and recited." Isaac Williams was amazed at Keble's mastery of poetry, and told his tutor so. The tutor said : " John Keble may understand Aristotle, but he knows nothing of poetry. It is not his line."

He was detained at Oxford, again by seeming chance, after the vacation had begun, and Keble called on him. He told Keble that he had made no plans for holiday reading, and Keble, after a few moments' thought, said, to his astonishment: "I am going to leave Oxford now for good. Suppose you come and read with me. The Provost has asked me to take Robert Wilberforce, and I declined, but, if you would come, you might be companions." How little Keble dreamed that his generous offer (for it was to be at his own charges) was to save a sinner, nay more, give a saint to an unborn Movement which should save the Church. Isaac Williams says: "If a merciful God had miraculously interposed to arrest my course, I should not have had a stronger assurance of His Presence, than I have always had in looking back to that day." During this memorable vacation he made friends with Froude, as I have described in the preceding chapter, but it was Keble who converted him by his sheer goodness. "Religion a reality, and a man wholly made up of love, with charms of conversation, thought, and kindness, beyond what one had experienced among boyish companions—this broke in upon me all at once."

The friendship with Froude, begun at Southrop, ripened later at Oxford. Isaac Williams was changing rapidly. Where he had been idle he was now studious; where he had been prominent he became retiring; where he had been merry-hearted he became consumed by shame and sorrow. He fell into a new set of friends. Once he met Newman at breakfast with a Fellow. This meeting impressed itself on his mind, but Newman could never remember it. Newman ignored him, and the conversation turned " on the subject of serving churches, and how much they would allow him for a Sunday." Newman, he observes, seemed less refined then than when he knew him later " in the Movement."

About 1825 Isaac Williams broke down through over-study, and consulted an eminent doctor, who forbade him to read any books. It was singularly unfortunate advice, as cessation from study made him more introspective than ever, but he recovered sufficiently to be ordained to a quiet curacy in 1829. He returned to Oxford as a Fellow in 1831, two years before the Movement began, and through Froude became the friend of Newman, whom he was to serve later as curate at Littlemore.

The Movement engaged his pen very soon, and he wrote poems in the *Lyra Apostolica* and some of the *Tracts for the Times*. He dined daily with Newman, and took long walks with him, and watched his Churchmanship ripening, but he seems to have maintained a fine independence of mind which should deter the superficial student of this revolutionary Movement from regarding him as a kind of Boswell to Dr. Johnson. Such an impression might arise in the mind from the fact that he was not a spear-head. He appears in every page of the history, but rather as an armour-bearer, or, to be more modern in one's simile, as the holder of coats at a street fight. Such a view would not do him justice. From the outset, though he was deeply fond of Newman, he was quick to observe a subtle difference between him and Froude and Keble. The Keble tradition set score upon character rather than intellect, so prized by the school of Whately. He observed in Newman, who had been a disciple of Whately's before Keble changed him, an intellect as restless as his character was beautiful. He enjoyed his quiet work with him at St. Mary's and Littlemore, but as time went on withdrew as much as he could.

We lived daily very much together, but I had a secret uneasiness, not from anything said or implied, but from a want of repose about his character, that I thought he would start into something different from Keble and Pusey, though I knew not in what direction it would be. Often after walking together, when leaving him, have I heard a deep secret sigh which I could not interpret. It seemed to speak of weariness of the world, and of aspirations for something he wished to do and had not yet done. Of the putting out of Church principles he often spoke as of an experiment which he did not know whether the Church of England would bear, and knew not what would be the issue.

This reflective and sober parson, who shrank from the dramatic in Newman, was, however, to be the cause of a great explosion which almost wrecked the Movement. His Tract 80, *On Reserve in Communicating Religious Knowledge* (*vide* my chapter on Newman for a discussion of " Reserve "), appeared in 1839. Bishops denounced it, in some cases without having read it, and churchfolk who had a little sympathy only with the Movement scuttled away like hunted rabbits, and those who distrusted the Movement held up hands in holy horror and said : " We always said so." Its title was admittedly unfortunate, suggesting " a love of secret and crooked ways," although its aim was to prevent a careless use of sacred words and phrases.

In 1842 Isaac Williams, who had withdrawn his candidature for the Poetry Professorship vacated by Keble in consequence of bitter opposition, retired to a country parsonage. Although three terrific years were to tick away before Newman went, he had in part foreseen the *débâcle*, distrustful of the new party that had cut across the Movement, seeking to deflect it from sober Anglican principles ; and now made it his own contribution to produce only *Devotional Commentaries* in the Keble tradition. But his genius for friendship triumphed over tragedy, and he, almost alone among the Tractarians, kept in touch with Newman after '45. A few letters that have been preserved from Newman show how affectionately he regarded him, and how frank their correspondence was.

Of all human things [writes Newman in 1863] perhaps Oxford is nearest my heart,—and some parsonages in the country. I cannot ever realize to myself that I shall never see what I love so much again . . . but why should I wish to see what is no longer what I loved ? All things change ; the past never returns here. My friends, I confess, have *not* been kind. . . . I despond about the cause of dogmatic truth in England altogether. Who can tell what is before us ? The difficulty is that the arguments of infidelity are deeper than those of Protestantism, and in the same direction. (I am using Protestantism in the sense in which you and Pusey would agree in using it.) . . . Everything I hear makes me fear that latitudinarian opinions are spreading furiously in the Church of England. I grieve deeply at it. The Anglican Church has been a most useful breakwater against scepticism. The time might come when you as well as I might expect that it would be said above, "Why cumbereth it the ground?" but at present it upholds far more truth in England than any other form of religion would, and than the Catholic Roman Church could.

Their last meeting was singularly pathetic. In 1865 Newman stayed with him. Williams was in weak health. He had for years been a martyr to chronic asthma. He insisted on driving his guest to the station, and the exposure provoked the illness to which he succumbed. Newman wrote, on hearing of his death :

My first sad thought is that in a certain sense I have killed him. . . ! He has really been a victim of his old love for me. He has never lost sight of me—ever inquiring about me from others, sending messages, or writing to me. I so much feared he was overdoing himself—but he would not allow it. I wanted him to let me walk down, but he wanted to have more talk ; and then, when he set off, he could not say a word. . . . Poor John Keble, how will it be broken to him ?

Strange endings to beautiful friendships ! Impassable chasms between great men who, as they fared forth upon their quests, harked ever back to early days when hopes ran high, and a fair field was theirs for co-operative valour. Thoughts of what might have been. Unkind reality. A kindly but dimmer light gleaming through the darkness on weeping eyes. A future all unknown. The Catholic Movement is a romance of broken hearts.

Poor Isaac Williams in his parsonage, faithful to his friends to the end. Two poor, ageing men in the Oratory at Edgbaston, one of them lonely, conscious of the distrust of those to join whom he had left all, hungering for those whom he had left. Two cells, each with a bed, a desk and an altar. Mr. St. John. John Henry Newman.

As the latter held the sacred chalice, with its ruby content, at the Mass of Requiem " for his dear soul " (as he spoke of Isaac Williams) he must have known, with the knowledge that tender, priestly hearts have well, that the tears of Christ are commingled with the out-poured Blood, that the altar is a City of Refuge for all who love one another at a distance, whether it be the distance of memory, as the years roll by, or the distance of place, or the distance, the greatest distance of all, of religious difference.

To me the picture of Newman saying Mass for the repose of the soul of Isaac Williams is not only one of exquisite loveliness, but an earnest of what may be in store for the Catholic Church when a million Latin altars are bedewed by penitential tears over separation, as now are hundreds of Anglican altars.

VI

JOHN KEBLE
1792–1866

ON the Feast of St. Mark, in the year of grace
1792, a son was born to the parson of Fairford,
Gloucestershire, who was to transform the Anglican Communion, and shine as the brightest star in
her firmament.

Bright stars were needed, for the night was dark.
A deep torpor had fallen upon the Church, which
seemed like to die of senile decay. There were such
dense clouds of ignorance that the loveliness of
Keble's life was realized by few of his contemporaries. Fearful storms blotted out other stars, as
brilliant, as pure, as purposeful. But as they " went
out," he remained to turn many to righteousness,
and " shine as the stars for ever."

As a boy John Keble showed remarkable promise.
Unlike Newman and Faber, but like Pusey, he was
grounded in High Anglicanism. His father, who
had a leaning towards the Non-Jurors, and loathed
the Methodism of Wesley, taught him up to the age
of sixteen, when he was elected a student of Corpus
Christi College, Oxford. At the age of eighteen he

brilliantly carried off double first-class honours, hitherto the proud record of Sir Robert Peel. At nineteen he was made a Fellow of Oriel. Oriel College was the nursery of the Oxford Movement.

There he met Newman, whom he converted to Anglo-Catholicism. Newman had looked upon Keble as " something one would put under a glass and put on one's chimneypiece to admire, but as too unworldly for business," a superficial judgment that changed to ardent worship, as contact revealed new facets of his rock-like character, and communion the riches of his mind and soul.

Keble was, indeed, the meekest of men, but, like a famous forerunner in the Old Testament, was capable of fiery action, and possessed of an inflexible will. When a sacred cause or principle was at stake, it was safe in his hands. But he desired, and in part achieved, a measure of obscurity and quietness, for, though a brilliant scholar, he loved the quiet round of the country-side among simple folk more than all the dwellings of Oxford. And this has enhanced his fame, for he is regarded as the ideal country parish priest.

He inaugurated the Oxford Movement on July 14, 1833, with his Assize Sermon on National Apostasy; a sermon which, seemingly temperate, and awakening no storm at the moment, forms a chapter of Anglican history which can never be forgotten, although its occasion gave no promise of its permanence, as it was an outspoken topical criticism of Earl Grey's decision to suppress ten Irish bishoprics.

Thereafter there issued forth a cataract of Tracts, which earned for their writers the name of Tractarians. Of these Keble wrote only four, but his mind was behind them in an advisory capacity. His own literary contribution was of another sort. He was the poet of the Movement.

The Christian Year is still a living volume, and some of its hymns, such as " Sun of my soul " and " New every morning is the love," are sung wherever the sun sets and rises. He composed many of the poems while walking along the country lanes, and it was his wish to have them published only after his death. His father, however, pleaded for immediate publication, and he yielded. Thus *The Christian Year* appeared in 1827, anonymously, and became the Herald of the Movement. Where the Tracts angered the intellect, *The Christian Year* won the heart, and churchfolk began to imbibe Catholic principles with criticism disarmed by the gentle music of its poetry.

There were exceptions, of course. A sister of Dean Stanley had seceded to Rome, after heroic service in the Crimea, where Anglican and Roman Catholic Sisters combined in a work of mercy. He wrote :

My sister, whose exertions at the naval hospital at Tgerapia, have, I sincerely believe, been as free from any sectarian bias, as truly national and Christian, and as

71

universally good in their efforts as it was possible for those of any human being to be, was stopped the other day by the Chaplain. He begged to have five minutes' conversation with her. He felt responsible for the publications circulated in the hospital, and he had found one of a very improper character : parts of it he highly disapproved ; parts of it he did not understand. She asked to see it. It was a *Christian Year* left by one of the ladies with a sick midshipman. In consequence of this he preached against them next Sunday in their presence, as " creeping in unawares, etc."

Bishop Westcott once wrote :

Keble, Wordsworth, Goethe. Is not the first the true poet ; the second, a poet who felt that he had a mission to perform, but commenced from nature instead of revelation ; the third, a sad example of those who, " though they might half heaven reveal, by idol hymns profane the sacred soul-enthralling strain " ?

But this was exaggerated praise. Keble was a genuine poet, and reached a measure of perfection within his sphere, but his inspiration was occasional. He was primarily a great priest who in his days pleased the Lord, whose many talents were consecrated to the high and holy task of recalling English Churchmen to the Faith which saints believed of old.

Like all the Tractarians, he was sober and disciplined. His parishioners would meet him reading his Bible on his daily round of visitation, and were so profoundly influenced that it seemed to observers as if all in Hursley, where he settled soon after his marriage in the autumn of 1835 (a marriage which vastly annoyed Newman), went about singing " Holy, Holy, Holy " all day long. He rebuilt Hursley church out of royalties from *The Christian Year*, of which over one hundred thousand copies were sold in twenty-six years. He loved children, and his catechizings in church were unforgettable. Like Charles Kingsley he organized Sunday cricket. " The youthful villagers," writes an old parishioner, " played, and the elder ones with the mothers and babies sat and looked on. The two village inns . . . were kept by most respectable men, both of them communicants and in the choir."

It must not be imagined, however, that his even round was undisturbed by opposition. His bishop for many years refused to ordain his deacon a priest, and he was drawn into all the storms and turmoils of the ecclesiastical times.

In 1863 he went to Bournemouth, where he died on March 29, 1866, from paralysis. He was buried at Hursley, whither went a mighty company of Churchmen to pay such homage as revealed the immensity of his influence.

For several generations that influence continued to be felt not only in the drawing-rooms of the upper classes but in their nurseries, through the consecrated art of Charlotte Mary Yonge, his close friend, whom he had prepared for confirmation and encouraged to embark upon a literary career which, in the *Daisy Chain* and many old, fragrant tales, taught children

" how intimately creed and character are intertwined." For forty years she edited the *Monthly Packet*, a magazine which exercised a profound influence in Church circles. With the proceeds of the *Daisy Chain* she built the first *Southern Cross* for the Melanesian Mission, whose magnificent and (literally) palatial successor was a short while ago consecrated and launched.

Although the Anglican Communion chooses now, *officially*, to recognize his centenary, he, in whose memory Keble College stands, was unhonoured while he lived. He was never offered any preferment save a colonial Archdeaconry, and was regarded with disdain and dislike by many pompous bishops and clergy whose names are well forgotten. If the Anglican Communion had not shelved her power to canonize it is safe to say that John Keble would be the first of the latter-day saints to adorn the Kalendar. He never despaired when days were darkest, and his calm continuance in well-doing is a lasting rebuke to those who faint and fall in the stress of persecution.

EDWARD BOUVERIE PUSEY
1800–1882

TO the modern Catholic Dr. Pusey looms through the mist of time as an austere giant, who did great works, and was a scholar of monstrous learning, and revived conventual life in the Church of England, and gave a name to the Movement other than " Tractarian " (for Anglo-Catholics, as they designated *themselves*, were often called " Puseyites "). But he seems so lofty, lonely, austere, self-disciplined, so aloof from enthusiasms, so sober as a judge, to the young so elderly and to the aged so heroic, that he is, as it were, taken for read. Such is the writer's own confession, who has now begun to worship the heroic doctor of the Church, and to discern the humble, tender heart torn by the changes and chances of the great revival.

Edward Bouverie Pusey was born of noble parents on August 22, 1800, and imbibed Catholic principles at his mother's knee. There were nine children. From his paternal ancestors, the Bouveries of the sixteenth century, he inherited a tendency to originate enterprise, capacity to organize, and an indomitable and hopeful perseverance. A weakly, delicate boy, quiet and retiring, he was fonder of books than of games, and always wished to become a clergyman. In 1823, Eton and Christ Church days all over, the march of life begun, he was elected a Fellow of Oriel, and then, with remarkable prescience of troublous days in store, which few foresaw, began with indefatigable industry to fit himself to stand, and help others to stand, against the breakers of scepticism which, gathering force in Germany, were to roll over Christianity. He learnt German. He learnt Arabic, Syriac and Chaldee, often working sixteen hours a day with frail health. In 1827 he had become the most learned scholar in England, with a European reputation. He was rewarded by being appointed Regius Professor of Hebrew at Oxford, a post which he held for fifty-four years, and received Holy Orders.

He had been awakened to a sense of danger by a long and barren correspondence with a young atheist. " I suppose," he wrote in later days, " I have read more infidel books than anyone living. I have read them until I flung them to the ground, sick with horror and loathing." But his fruitless effort to convert his tedious friend was a blessing in disguise. It gave him his first real experience of the deadly breath of infidel thought upon the soul. " It decided me," he said, " to devote my life to the Old Testament; as I saw that was the point of attack in our defences which would be most easily breached."

The Anglican Communion, the most learned of the

Churches as touching the Scriptures, to whom has been given the glory of vindicating the inspiration and essential truthfulness of the Bible, against the corrosive criticism of continental scholars, owes her victory, under God, to Edward Bouverie Pusey. He foresaw and he prepared. He wrote in 1878 to Dr. Liddon : " I can remember the room in Göttingen in which I was sitting when the real condition of religious thought in Germany flashed upon me." The enemy was Rationalism.

A very human Pusey was hidden beneath the sober scholar. He who, as he rose from his desk in young manhood, with aching eyes and cramped limbs, after hours of toil upon Arabic, could envy the bricklayers whom he saw through his window, endured, for over ten years, a heart hunger which few knew of. As a boy he had spent a few weeks at home in the summer of 1818. He was nearly eighteen. He met there the youngest daughter of an old Shropshire family, the Barkers. They were neighbours and friends of the Pusey family. Maria Raymond Barker was seventeen, and he fell head over heels in love with her at first sight. The parents intervened, as parents ever do, Mr. Barker from a desire to have his daughter accept a brilliant marriage which had been offered her, and Mr. Pusey from anxiety not to embarrass his friend. Unlike romances of this sort there was no opposition to the heavy fathers. The boy and girl separated sadly. For years young Pusey suffered a permanent and deep depression, and his health was seriously impaired. He became a martyr to head-aches. His sorrow grew more painful as the days went by. All joy was fled from home, though he remained a dutiful son. Maria Raymond Barker did not marry. She, too, had given her heart, and would not, could not, withdraw. Ten years passed by, and they met again and married. That was in 1828. Their married life was very beautiful. A quiverful of children made home happy. They entertained, and read together, and prayed together. Pusey's letters to his wife read like sermons, in which, with irritating reiteration, he laments his unworthiness to have so much happiness. Then she died, and he faced a future of lonely service. Newman, who cared so deeply for Pusey that he dared not tell him plainly that he was on his death-bed as an Anglican, went to see him on the morning of her death. Newman was the only friend Pusey saw. For many months he was inconsolable, and friends hardly dared to intrude.

One child of his marriage deserves remembrance. There is something as lovely as awful in Pusey's account of her death, in maidenhood. She had longed to devote her life to God, without reserve, and had seemed peculiarly gifted to that end, so much so that her father really expected her to leave her mark upon the Church, as many maiden saints have done. But she died after a lingering illness, in which, towards the end, she had reached out to acute suffer-ing, if by bearing it with fortitude she might come nearer God. Her wish was granted, for a sheer agony came upon her. Picture the lonely, anguished priest, alone in the death-chamber. We know from his words what happened.

Her dear eyes [he wrote] had turned up under her eyelids, as they do often in dying persons . . . and the sobs had become fainter and I had been expecting the last gasp, when the cough returned and brought her to life . . . my heart sank within me . . . at last, all at once, her dear eyes, which had been half closed for hours, opened quite wide, and gazed with an earnest, longing look at something we did not see . . . they expanded and became full, larger and fuller than they ever were in health . . . and then she turned them full to me . . . and there was in them an unearthly lustre, and then there came over the mouth, which had been only sobbing . . . such a smile of joy and Divine love and triumph, that I never saw anything approaching to it on the earth. It was all wholly Heavenly. It spread gradually over her . . . lips . . . masking the expression of pain and absorbing it in Divine love ; it would have been a laugh of joy almost, only there was no sound. . . . I almost laughed for joy in return. . . .

He then goes on :

It is a very solemn thing which I am going to say, but it is so wholly unlike anything of this earth, or in herself, and something so Divine, that I cannot describe it in words, though I have no doubt that she saw into the unseen world—perhaps our Blessed Lord Himself, Whose coming we had so often prayed for, and that her countenance caught the light to which she was approaching. . . . Of this I feel quite certain, that it was something Divine, and a special vouchsafement to her.

Dare one hope that when (and in the fullness of time it must come about) the Anglican Communion regains a capacity to canonize saints, this story may be remembered, and his authority accepted who was the instrument chosen by Divine Providence for the restoration of the Religious life?

I have digressed in order to show the humanity of the great Doctor, and perhaps may be excused for recording another incident, to show his self-control. He and his wife had somewhat impoverished themselves by giving £5,000 to the Bishop of London's fund for the building of churches, an act of self-denial which necessitated rigid economy, and the giving up of horses and carriage. As if that were not enough he inaugurated a scheme, after Mrs. Pusey's death, for the building of St. Saviour's church, Leeds. He provided the money anonymously, and gave, also, a beautiful chalice and paten in memory of his daughter. It was to be used for the first time at the consecration of the church. Bishop Longley, full of tedious tiresomeness, at length consented to consecrate the church, and came expecting riots, nervously suspicious of the appointments of the church and the order of service. The Rev. J. B. Mozley wrote of this event:

The Bishop . . . was dreadfully nervous and, in fact, one would suppose Pusey was a lion, or some beast of prey, people seem to have been so afraid of him. The Bishop was afraid of being entrapped into anything, and objected to this and that. Among the rest, he saw on one of the doors the sentence—" Pray for the sinner who built this church," and required evidence that the sinner was *alive* before he consecrated.[1]

He refused to use the plate, because it contained a prayer for the repose of the soul of Lucy Pusey. An eye-witness said that he should never forget the look of suffering on Dr. Pusey's face—" the more striking from its still and almost stern composure."

We must retrace our steps. Pusey had not been associated with the Movement at the outset, but came in with an important Tract on Fasting, to which he appended his initials. That gave to a suspected " mob " prestige and power. He was soon an object of persecution. On May 14, 1843, ten years after the Movement had begun, he preached a sermon on the Holy Eucharist before the University. He had written a Tract on Baptism (really a treatise) whose verity he was anxious to soften by a course of sermons on " Comforts to the Penitent." He considered that the first sermon, if upon the Holy Eucharist, would be unexceptionable. He never made a greater mistake. It was a quiet, uncontroversial sermon, entirely in accord with the teaching of the Anglican Church, as expressed in the Prayer Book and the writings of her great Divines. Dean Church has recorded that it was " a high Anglican sermon, full, after the example of the Homilies, Jeremy Taylor, and the devotional writers like George Herbert and Bishop Ken, of the fervid

[1] An unprincipled bishop, for a graven prayer for one alive must in course of time become a prayer for a soul departed !

language of the Fathers; and that was all. Beyond this it did not go: its phraseology was strictly within Anglican limits." One of Pusey's colleagues accused the sermon of heresy before the Vice-Chancellor, who chose six doctors of divinity to judge it (one being the accuser!) No opportunity was given to Pusey to speak in his own defence. The sermon was denounced, and he was suspended from preaching in the University for two years.

The crooked methods which his accusers used to justify themselves in the eyes of a shocked University were not known for many years, until Liddon found them out from papers, because they had tricked Pusey into a promise of silence, and then taken advantage of him. He sealed his lips, though he could have pulverized his persecutors by a word. The chapters upon this score in the standard volumes are an interesting revelation of clerical knavery, and of Pusey's much-abused trust in his fellow-men. To make matters worse, he had kept no copies of his own letters, and when he begged for their return for a few days was curtly refused the favour. An address of protest was sent to Dr. Wynter, the Vice-Chancellor, by 230 non-resident members of Convocation, the third and fourth names appended to it being those of Gladstone and Judge Coleridge. It deprecated " that construction of the Statute under which Dr. Pusey has been condemned; which, contrary to the general principles of justice, subjects a person to penalties without affording him the means of explanation or defence." The Vice-Chancellor sent a furious reply to London by the University Bedel, with the address, which he refused to receive.

Two years later Pusey patiently took up his parable where he had laid it down, and reiterated, more in the language of the Prayer Book than of the Fathers, the principles enunciated in his condemned sermon.

Newman's secession was Pusey's veriest, sharpest purgatory. When the threefold cord, of Newman, Keble and Pusey, was broken, Pusey's heart was broken. If, many years on, Newman was discovered in tears at Littlemore, Pusey wept dry-eyed the long years through. He had made Newman his confidant, had referred all matters of moment to him, and trusted him to come out of the dark night of doubtfulness into the clear shining of the day he himself walked in. Newman felt this poignantly, and his letters are a study in reserve. He threw out hints, but they were not understood. He corresponded less frequently in order to give less pain. It was probably Pusey's influence which kept him in the Anglican Communion until '45. Pusey rose magnificently, with wistful patience, to the task that Newman's secession thrust upon him. His view of that is of great interest after ninety years of wounding and weakening secessions. He wrote, a little before the event, to Keble, who had been wondering with the Anglican Archdeacon Manning (afterwards Cardinal) whether Newman's secession, should it come about, might not be less damaging if he went to Rome to make it:

I have myself looked upon this of dear N. as a mysterious dispensation, as though (if it indeed be so) Almighty God was drawing him, as a chosen instrument for some office in the Roman Church (although he himself goes, of course, not as a reformer, but as a simple act of faith) . . . at least I have come into this way of thinking since I have realized to myself that it was likely to be thus. But others who look at a distance think it is only the beginning for us all. . . .

And so it might have proved had not he written a pastoral to the sheep when the shepherd was smitten, which allayed many fears, and saved the Movement from collapse. I have space only for a noble passage :

The first pang came to me years ago, when I had no other fear, but heard that he was prayed for by name in so many churches and religious houses on the Continent. The fear was suggested to me, " If they pray so earnestly for this object, that he may soon be an instrument of God's glory among them, while among us there is so much indifference, and in part dislike, may it not be that their prayers may be heard, that God will give them whom they pray for—we forfeit whom we desire not to retain ? " . . .

In my deepest sorrow at the distant anticipation of our loss, I was told of the saying of one of their most eminent historians, who owned that they were entirely unequal to meet the evils with which they were beset, that nothing could meet them but some movement which should infuse new life into their Church, and that for this he looked to one man, and that N. I cannot say what a ray of comfort darted into my mind. It made me at once realize more both that what I dreaded might be, and its end. With us he was laid aside. . . . Our Church has not known how to employ him. And, since this was so, it seemed as if a sharp sword were lying in its scabbard, or hung up in the sanctuary, because there was no one to wield it. . . . He seems then to me not so much gone from us as transplanted into another part of the vineyard, where the full energies of his powerful mind can be employed, which here they were not. . . . It is perhaps the greatest event which has happened since the Communion of the Churches has been interrupted. . . .

And to Newman he wrote :

You will pray the more for us, who are left to struggle on in a stormy sea with the winds contrary—altho', I trust, with His secret Presence—for us, both individually and as a body, that we may be visibly, too, one fold under One Shepherd. . . . Ah, past and future is one intense mystery. God be with you always, and remember me a sinner.

We know what Rome did with the sharp, shining sword—how it put purple jewels upon it, but used it not where the battle was fiercest, where men and women were losing faith in God Himself, and cared not for ecclesiastical controversy ! We know, alas ! that the secession of many sons and daughters of *Ecclesia Anglicana* to the Rock whence admittedly she was hewn has not softened it towards us.

Dr. Pusey's attitude to Rome was always sane and sanguine, although he was ever deeply conscious of the barriers that divided the two Communions. He wrote a famous " Eirenicon," an olive branch discharged from a catapult, unfortunately, in 1865, in reply to an attack by Cardinal Manning, and Newman replied to it, to his disappointment. He looked forward, with touching hope, to the Vatican Council of 1869, being persuaded that such a gathering of Bishops could not fail to be guided towards peace by the Holy Spirit. Its decrees, however, crushed him, and thereafter he took no active part in efforts for Reunion. " The Vatican Council," he wrote, " was the greatest sorrow I ever had in a long life."

No priest heard more confessions than Dr. Pusey; nor was one exposed to such universal disapprobation; or so humble and self-disciplined. Dr. Pusey's austerities are worthy to be remembered in modern days by priests who have, perhaps, become so overwhelmed by activities that activity of soul has been diminished. If modern Anglo-Catholics have a gay lilt in their lives, they certainly lack that austerity which commended the Tractarians to the earnest folk of the times.

He ate distasteful food; wore a hair shirt next his skin; used the discipline on his body; accepted humiliations with the eagerness of a saint; said Mass every day at four; ignored malaise and headaches; made acts of humiliation when servants touched their caps to him; and had a rule of life " always to lie down in bed, confessing that I am unworthy to lie down except in Hell, but, so praying, to lie down in the Everlasting Arms." To look into his face was to see the light of Heaven. Thus his sermons were listened to by breathless congregations, in spite of their inordinate length and his monotonous delivery.

He died on September 16, 1882, at the age of eighty-two. To quote a recent writer:

Pusey's influence on the Catholic Revival was profound, unique, and lasting. He did not possess the intellectual brilliance of Newman, or the winning charm of Keble, but he had a rock-like stability and power of self-forgetfulness which Newman lacked, and a capacity for leadership to which Keble could make no claim. . . .

His life, said Mr. G. W. E. Russell,

combined all the elements of moral grandeur—an absolute and calculated devotion to a sacred cause ; a child-like simplicity ; and a courage which grew more buoyant as the battle thickened. Its results are written in the Book of Record which lies before the Throne of God.

VIII

CHARLES MARRIOTT
1811–1858

THE most pathetic hero of the Oxford Movement, Charles Marriott, is the more worthy of remembrance in the " Keble " year, 1933, because, unlike the famous men whose names are household words among Churchmen, he has been forgotten, though with Pusey he held the fort when Newman went out in the forties, rallied the scattered forces and saved the Oxford Movement from complete collapse.

He was the son of John Marriott, a polished and accomplished country parson and felicitous writer of hymns, whose " God, that madest earth and heaven " and " Thou, whose Almighty Word," are sung all the world over. Charles learned his letters from the village schoolmaster, and showed a voracious appetite, while very young, for reading all sorts of subjects. His brother wrote :

I well recollect the satisfaction my Father used to express at his rapid progress in learning. His childhood gave promise of his great powers. He very early acquired the habit of thinking out subjects for himself ; and used to form his own conclusions with great distinctness, and often with a degree of judgment far above his years, on matters of difficulty and importance . . . he showed singular aptitude in acquiring languages. When quite a child he preferred reading . . . to the out-of-door amusements which occupy the leisure of most boys : never happier than when ensconced behind the window-curtain (where he could sit unobserved and unmolested) he was devouring the *Encyclopædia Britannica.*

To those early browsings in the venerable volumes of the *Encyclopædia* must be attributed his vast knowledge of out-of-the-way subjects. He seemed able to discourse on anything, and his retentive memory became an Encyclopædia in itself.

When taken with the children to see Exeter Cathedral [wrote a cousin], while the elder ones were trying to measure the circumference of the great bell with bits of string, Charles was heard from behind to deliver (in his small peculiar voice) the oracular counsel : "Take the diameter."

He was evidently a boy with a sacrificial outlook on life, because he neither spent nor saved his money, and he never seemed to have any. When his parents left Broad Clyst, there was a loud wail from the old almswomen who lived near the Parsonage gate. They said that they should miss Master Charles as "he always brought them his money of a Saturday." His mother died in 1821, and his father four years later. The orphan boy of fourteen went to live with an aunt at Rugby, and when she married his father's former curate, became his pupil in a

Shropshire rectory until he was old enough to go to Exeter College, Oxford.

His immense knowledge was soon noticed there, and I am indebted to him for illuminating one of the minor problems of my life. It was remarked that it was strange that anyone should have thought of educating fleas, and, anyway, how in the world did they do it. Marriott looked up from the book he was reading, and said: "The first thing to be done is to put them in a pill-box, till they are quite tired of jumping." His memory was amazing. After reading a difficult poem by Wordsworth, of 135 lines, once through, and glancing at it a second time, he repeated the whole by heart.

Such was the intellectual quality of the man who at Oriel became the office-boy of the Oxford Movement. His immense gifts were wasted because he had the faculty of attracting all the odd jobs that arise from vast literary undertakings, such as the *Library of the Fathers*. While he should have been creating books which would have become of permanent value to the Church, he found himself burdened by an immense and unmanageable correspondence, visitors at all hours, miles (I use the word intentionally) of proofs, intricate indexes, which could have been compiled by lesser folk, and the tedious task of correcting the translations of others. Marriott and the *Library of the Fathers* went together unto his life's end. They were a halter, however, that he bore gladly, for he had no life apart from the " Movement," and seemed to

regard the office of Gibeonite as appointed for him by
Divine Providence. He is a warning to those who
have too many things to do, and thereby fail to use
gifts fully which they alone may possess.

The immense amount of work which he accumu-
lated was made the more impossible by his untidi-
ness. Marriott's room was a ghastly, everlasting
muddle. Books were everywhere. To sit down, a
visitor had to take a heap of precious tomes off a chair,
and put it on the floor. His shelves were thick with
dust. There were letters everywhere, and his fine
memory for facts seemed to break down completely
in his domestic circle. There is a delicious account
of one of his entertainments in Burgon's *Twelve
Good Men*.

An American Bishop . . . attended by three of his
clergy, having crossed the Atlantic, would present himself
at Marriott's door—who instantly asked them all four to
breakfast next morning, and sent off cards by his servant
to certain of his intimates. . . . On his way from Hall
or Chapel—or in the street—he would ask another, and
another, and another. . . . Unfortunately he kept no
reckoning. The result may be imagined. On entering
the dear man's rooms next morning, whereas breakfast
had been laid for ten, fifteen guests had assembled already.
While we were secretly counting the tea-cups, another
rap was heard, and in came two University Professors.
All laughed : but it was no laughing matter, for still
another and another person presented himself. The bell
was again and again rung : more and more tea and coffee,
—muffins and dry toast,—butter and bread,—cream and
eggs,—chops and steaks,—were ordered ; and " Richard "

was begged to " spread my other table-cloth on my other table." The consequence was that our host's violoncello, —fiddle-strings and music-books,—printer's proofs and postage stamps,—medicine bottles and pill-boxes,— respirator and veil,—grey wrapper for his throat and green shade for his eyes,—pamphlets and letters innumer- able,—*all* were discharged in a volley on to the huge sofa. At last . . . (thanks to Richard's superhuman exertions) twenty of us (more or less) sat down to break- fast. . . . I am bound to say that the meal was an entire success,—as far as the strangers were concerned. They were greatly entertained,—in more senses than one. There was plenty of first-rate conversation too. Good humour certainly prevailed universally. The delightful absurdity of the whole proceeding was so painfully conspicuous, and the experience (to strangers) so unique ! . . . But oh the consequences of such a *scrimmage* to the poor overworked student when the guests were gone, and the serious business of the day had to commence ! Chaos must first be reduced to order :—the letters must be read and answered :—the proof sheets scrutinized and annotated :—there would be callers to attend to :—bores to encounter :—engagements to keep. And long before *that*, the second post would have come in, and perhaps another batch of " illustrious strangers " would have announced their arrival.

Such was the man who, broken-hearted when his beloved John Henry Newman went out, stepped into the gap and rallied the forces. He had studied every- thing : higher mathematics and astronomy ; music and singing ; poetry, biography, history, metaphysics, Irvingism, astrology, the habits of fleas, stars, and comets ; logic ; political economy, ontology ;

Utilitarianism ; agriculture and I know not what.
One thing he had studied more than all else—how to
be a good priest. So, when the cholera epidemic
was at its height, he would be found far from his
proofs and Fathers, at the beds of the dying. The
noble picture of the tired saint shriving a poor man
at one bed, while a Roman Catholic priest per-
formed a like task at the next, is one of the clearest
proofs that the Oxford Movement was not an
academic whimsy. All this, too, with health so
frail that he had not been able to retain his post, in
early life, as the first Principal of Chichester Theological College.

Possessed of some means, he made himself poor.
To help Newman financially, after his secession, and
perhaps to prevent him from establishing a Latin
community in the cottages at Littlemore, he bought
them from him, and established a printing press.
He ought to have been prevented by his friends
because, while it was certainly a useful asset to the
Movement, the practical details were beyond his scope.
One day he would toil out to Littlemore heavily laden
with new type ; another he would write hastily, to
keep the press employed ; a third he would over-order
miles of paper, while all the time he should have been
using his remarkable gifts in studious employ. It was
a pathetic tragedy, and it killed him.

His importance, at the time of the crisis, cannot be
over-estimated, though he had no gifts for leadership.
Burgon says :

Never was there a time when . . . calmness and intrepidity were more needed. . . . Hugh James Rose had been for three years removed from the scene. . . . Keble was far away at his country cure. Pusey was the only leader at head-quarters : and to him Marriott opportunely joined himself. He brought to the cause every good and perfect gift . . . above all things, a well-merited reputation for sound Theological learning and solid Classical attainment,—combined with what I can only designate as a truly Apostolic holiness of character,— a most conciliatory, sympathizing disposition,—entire singleness of purpose. But his prime qualification for supplying Newman's place was his unswerving loyalty to the Church of his fathers. . . . His view of what constitutes a living branch of Christ's Holy Catholic Church soared far above the region of logical quibbles, intellectual subtleties,—arbitrary definitions, irrelevant truisms. It was the view of Andrewes and of Hooker —of Laud and of Bull—of Barrow and of Bramhall,— of Pearson and of Butler,—of Rose and of Mill.

He died, after a long illness, on September 15, 1858, at the age of forty-seven. But for him, humanly speaking, the Anglo-Catholic Movement would not be keeping a Centenary.

IX

FREDERICK WILLIAM FABER
1814–1863

THE church at Elton, Huntingdonshire; the evening of Sunday, November 16, 1845. Contrary to custom, there has been no early celebration, and the parishioners wonder why. Perhaps their parish priest will tell them. They do not grumble, for they worship the ground he treads on. In their simple way they regard him as the final authority in all things spiritual.

When he agreed to become their pastor, in the autumn of 1842, many of them were living in sin. Their village was notorious. He himself wrote soon after taking up residence: "I have tumbled into a sad parish; eight hundred people, and nearly four hundred *rabid* Dissenters, who have found out that I am, to use the expression of a hostile churchwarden, tainted, to say the least, with Puseyism." And again: "I have nearly one thousand people here, and *everything* wants doing. But I have no right to complain: the Dissenters are very violent: they *worship* the Sabbath, and really, though they seem to cheat and live impurely on week-days, none of their neighbours seems to doubt that they are *the* elect. . . ."

In a short while Faber has fulfilled many days. The chapel bells call a scanty few, for he has emptied the chapels. The " Sabbath Day " is no longer a weekly occasion for sin, for he has thrown open his grounds, and cleaned up the place by cricket and football. The altar is thronged, and so, more surprisingly, is the confessional. He has overcome prejudice by definiteness tempered by engaging presentation. And he practises more than he preaches. Beneath his clothes he wears a knotted horse-hair cord as a perpetual penance. He is known to eat barely anything—a herring and a few potatoes only for dinner. He has fainted at prayers through hunger.

His rectory is a sort of monastery, because he has influenced the youths of the village so strongly that a number of them meet regularly at midnight for the recitation of psalms ; practise auricular confession ; make their Communions frequently ; and on Fridays and other days, and every night in Lent, flagellate one another.

These " goings on at the rectory," which normally would, were they practised, have scandalized villagers and led to riots (there are riots in these days, alas ! over matters trivial compared with such Popery), have helped to convert them, and the powers of darkness are indignant. Mysterious noises resound through the rectory, often just outside the door where the little community is engaged in prayer; and diligent and immediate search with lights reveals nothing.

On the evening I am describing, the people of Elton have made their way to church along dark lanes and through the quiet village. The church is a home they love to visit; and the musical voice of the burly priest, whose face to look upon is beautiful by reason of his sanctity, is one they could listen to for hours. Sunday at Elton now brings many Pilgrims of the Night towards the Heavenly Jerusalem, where the voice of Jesus sounds like bells far off at even pealing.

To-night a light shall be quenched in their midst; a light whose clear shining has given them courage to turn their feet to God. How overwrought Mr. Faber seems! thinks a churchwarden anxiously. What can be amiss? He puts on his surplice and ascends the pulpit. He speaks haltingly a few preliminary words and then . . .

Not a sound comes from the congregation. They sit as if struck dead. What is their pastor saying? They cannot believe their ears. He tells them that all he has taught them is true, but that it is not the teaching of their Mother Church; that the Church has disavowed them, and that he must go where truth is to be found. He ends abruptly, stumbles down the stairs, throws his surplice [1] on the ground and leaves

---

[1] I have seen its neck-band, bearing his name in faded ink.

the church. No one moves for a while. Then a few go to the rectory, to tell him that he may preach whatever he chooses if only he will stay.

What a night of horror for Elton! A plague or a pestilence or a famine could be more easily borne; they could have understood had their shepherd been removed by promotion or death. To lose him thus! It is incomprehensible.

Many of them sit up all night, crouching over dying embers that symbolized, as it were, the dying of their interests, perhaps of their spiritual life. But their love for Mr. Faber cannot die. And so at dawn, hearing that he may depart at that hour, they assemble at their windows, and as with a few servants and young men bent on accompanying him into an unknown future, he passes for the last time by the old weather-worn houses, they wave handkerchiefs from the lattice windows under the crinkled roofs, or stand upon the uneven doorsteps to salute him. "God bless you, Mr. Faber," they cry, "wherever you go, God bless you."

Thus closed for ever a remarkable effort, in an age of religious deadness, to conduct an Anglican parish in the spirit of St. Philip and St. Alphonso. Faber would have said that it was pouring old wine into a new bottle (if I may invert the scriptural simile), but my comment is this. The startling success of his work shows clearly that there is Catholic soil in the Anglican Church for such flowers to take root and fructify, even for a season.

FREDERICK WILLIAM FABER

Frederick William Faber was the seventh child in a family of Huguenot origin. He was born on June 28, 1814, at the Vicarage of Calverley, in the West Riding of Yorkshire, where his grandfather was incumbent. His father soon afterwards became the Bishop of Durham's secretary. As a child he showed much nascent talent. " Ardent and impulsive," says a biographer, " he entered upon everything, whether work or play, with eagerness and determination ; and whatever he took up was invested in his eyes with an importance which led him to speak of it in somewhat exaggerated language." He was educated at the Grammar School of Bishop Auckland, and then privately in Westmorland. The impression of its beauties was never effaced from his mind, as we can see from his lines :

> Each hazel copse, each greenly tangled bower,
> Is sacred to some well-remembered hour ;
> Some quiet hour when nature did her part,
> And worked her spell upon my childish heart.

At the age of eleven he proceeded to Shrewsbury School, and thence, shortly afterwards, to Harrow, where his headmaster was Dr. Longley, afterwards Archbishop of Canterbury, whose friendship he always treasured. Here he devoted himself to English literature to the detriment of classical studies. In the Lent Term of the year that saw the birth of the Oxford Movement (1833) he went up to Balliol. A contemporary wrote :

99

Our first recollection of F. Faber is of a graceful and intelligent boy just launched into a great public school; and next, as a young man who had lately won for himself a high place in honours at Oxford. No one could have known him in those days without being attracted by a grace of person and mind rarely to be met with.

His religious ideas at this period were strongly Calvinistic, yet tempered by a trustful love of God one is not wont to associate with the shocking doctrine of Geneva. In one of his hymns, " The God of my childhood," he writes :

> They bade me call Thee Father, Lord !
> Sweet was the freedom deemed ;
> And yet more like a mother's ways
> Thy quiet mercies seemed.

He fell under the sway of Newman in St. Mary's and became a Tractarian, eagerly looking forward to the time when he could be ordained, although he was not without intellectual misgivings some years later as to the tenability of the Tractarian position. He offered his services in 1837 to the compilers of the " Library of the Fathers," and was assigned the translation of the Books of St. Optatus, and thus came to know Newman personally. In that year, too, he formed a friendship with Wordsworth, during a vacation at Ambleside. They often composed poems as they wandered together over the mountains of the Lake country. When he was ordained deacon (August 6, 1837) Wordsworth said : " I do not say you are wrong, but England loses a poet." For two years he worked at Ambleside and at Oxford, being made a priest on May 26, 1839 (by strange coincidence the Roman Feast of St. Philip Neri).

That summer he went on the Continent and returned with a contempt for Roman Catholic clergy. But the Continent cast a spell over him, and he made extensive journeys, saturating himself in Roman Catholicism. Prior to taking up work at Elton he went abroad again. "The last four years," writes a biographer, "had brought about a great change in his feelings towards the Catholic Church; and it was now more as a learner than as a critic that he intended to study her operations. He had a new source of interest in the inquiry; for the office which he was about to assume made him anxious to gather hints for the work which it would impose." During his travels he was several times on the point of being received into the Latin Church.

He was received by the Pope.

The Pope was perfectly alone, without a courtier or prelate, standing in the middle of the library, in a plain, white cassock, and a white silk skull-cap . . . he held out his hand, but I kissed his foot; there seemed to be a mean puerility in refusing the customary homage. With Dr. Baggs for interpreter, we had a long conversation; he spoke of Dr. Pusey's suspension, for defending the Catholic doctrine of the Eucharist, with amazement and disgust; he said to me, "You must not mislead yourself in wishing for unity, yet waiting for your *Church* to move. Think of the salvation of your own soul." I said I feared self-will and *individual* judging. He said,

" You are all individuals in the English Church. . . .
You must think for yourself and for your soul."

He gave him, then, a blessing, and Faber left in tears.

Pusey's condemnation at Oxford (described in
Chapter VII) would seem to have been the deter-
mining factor, really, in Faber's secession. He writes
of it thus :

> As to Pusey's business I feel an excessive indignation
> . . . in what a state of corruption our Church must be,
> when one of her four universities can suffer a board of
> doctors, without instant excommunication, to pass such
> a sentence ! . . . Where can the truth be authoritatively
> asserted ? How can the Church show it is not her sen-
> tence ? . . . As to myself, nothing retains me but the
> fear of self-will ; I grow more Roman every day, but I
> hope not wilfully. . . .

Soon afterwards he was praying at the shrine of
St. Aloysius on the feast of that Saint, and left the
church speechless, not knowing where he was going.

But he returned to take up pastoral duty at Elton,
an account of which I have given in my tale of
a surplice. I must add this. He had incurred heavy
debts at Elton, and knew that, if he seceded, he could
not meet them. Justice seemed to require him to stay
until he could pay his debtors. On the day he decided
to secede a friend who was hostile to Roman Catholicism sent him a cheque to pay his debts, saying that he
was distressed to think that such a barrier should come
between him and what he conceived to be his duty.

So he went out, accompanied by a few of his young

men, whom he formed into a lay community. He was shown much consideration in the Roman Catholic Church and founded the Oratory at Brompton, whose intensely Mediterranean character is due to his passion for Italy. His desire to Italianize England was not shared by Newman, and lack of sympathy tended in time to separate the London Oratory from the older establishment at Birmingham. Of this work I shall not write in detail. Faber was a great administrator, a winning preacher, a real saint. His health was shocking, but he worked prodigiously, and he wrote his books between Mass and breakfast.

If England lost a poet when Faber became an Anglican priest the Church gained a poet. Hymnody is the common heritage of Christendom, and many of his hymns are to be found in the books of all denominations. Sometimes they are the shadow of their original selves, hymns being peculiarly liable to mutilation, but no other Roman Catholic poet makes so universal an appeal. In the *English Hymnal* there are ten of his hymns, the most popular being : " O, come and mourn with me awhile " ; " Sweet Saviour, bless us ere we go " ; " Jesu, gentlest Saviour " (abridged) ; " Hark ! hark, my soul ! " and " There's a wideness in God's mercy."

He was a prolific writer of devotional books, with a charm all their own, the spirit of the poet enraptured by the beauties of nature breathing in every page. Who but a poet could have written thus ?

The sun sets on the twenty-fourth of December on the low roofs of Bethlehem, and gleams with wan gold on the steep of its stony ridge. The stars come out one by one. Time itself, as if sentient, seems to get eager, as though the hand of its angel shook as it draws on towards midnight. Bethlehem is at that moment the veritable centre of God's creation. How silently the stars drift down the steep of the midnight sky! Yet a few moments, and the Eternal Word will come.

Many do not care for Faber's style. As Mr. Chesterton is a master of paradox, so Faber was a master of exuberant description, often wandering into mazes of similes and contrasts, and heaping up adjectives until the reader feels shut in a superfluous hot-house in a tropical country. Yet a subtle loveliness makes much of it unforgettable.

Faber was not one of the causes of the Oxford Movement. He was a result. He was one of those who tried to deflect its course from the sober one laid down by the Tractarians. But his loss to the Anglican Church was grievous. Certainly he loved and served her faithfully, for, in spite of the Pope's exhortation, he waited two years before taking the irrevocable step, seeking to test her catholicity by his work at Elton.

He died on June 26, 1863.

With eyes full of a bright and joyous expression, as "the glory of God which was to fade away no more for ever began to dawn upon them, and the songs of heaven to break on his ears," he calmly passed away. The pilgrim of the night had been welcomed home at last by the angels of light.

St. Philip Neri had no more faithful son than he. He acquired his first devotion to him in 1843 when he visited the room in which the saint used to say Mass, in the Chiesa Nuova.

How little did I [he said in retrospect], a Protestant stranger in that room years ago, dream I should ever be of the Saint's family, or that the Oratorian father who showed it me should in a few years be appointed by the Pope the novice-master of the English Oratorians ! I remember how, when he kissed the glass of the case in which St. Philip's little bed is kept as a relic, he apologized to me as a Protestant, lest I should be scandalized, and told me with a smile how tenderly St. Philip's children loved their father. . . . If anyone had told me that in seven short years I should wear the same white collar in the streets of London . . . I should have wondered how anyone could dream so wild a dream.

When the Oratory was consecrated (an Oratorian told me) a Protestant went to the service and was afterwards shown over the building. " Who is that old man ? " he asked, pointing to a picture of St. Philip. " I saw him during the service, looking down from a balcony."

X

HENRY EDWARD MANNING
1808–1892

IN devoting this chapter to a leader of the Catholic Revival who passed from the Archdeaconry of Chichester to direct the fortunes of the Holy Roman Church in the thronged streets of London, and stand, if the assertion of a biographer is true, for a glittering moment on the steps of the Papal Throne, and turn from it in magnificent renunciation, I lay myself open to criticism. " How can you call Manning a ' Hero ' of the Oxford Movement," I may be asked, " when, sorely needed, he deserted it in the plenitude of his power, gave it a crushing blow ere it had recovered from that administered by Newman ; and returned to oppose it in an ultramontane temper that stiffened the veil of separation ; making the Movement appear but a nursery and hot-bed of Papalism ? "

Well, a precedent has been set by the inclusion of Newman and Faber, and I ascribe heroism as well to those who " went out " as to those who stayed.

The pain of secession must be weighed by a seceder's sensitiveness ; his environment ; his importance to others. To some, the act of secession is

a relief overweighing pain. To others, if filled with
the pastoral spirit, it is an agony. To others, again,
with few pastoral ties but many friendships, and a
love of old associations, secession causes the pain of
exile. Nowadays such pain is mitigated. A cleric
finds that he is not excluded by secession from fellowship with old friends. I have one in mind who,
having left the Anglican barque for Peter's, comes
back for social cruises. I meet him at Anglican
cocktail parties. He does not seem to have lost connexion. This could not be the case eighty years ago.
Secession, then, meant loss of everything held dear.
A seceder had to begin a new life, numbed by loss.
He was universally held to have sold the pass. He
was often ruined financially as well as socially. To
leave, then, was an act of heroism of a higher sort than
to stay, though the lesser suffering of staying was a
lasting one, while that of going was (save in such a
sensitive soul as Newman's) a spasm of exquisite agony
succeeded by healing and happiness.

However inadequate my excuses may seem, they
must serve, and I hope that my treatment may appease
my Anglican critics, for I propose to invert a pyramid,
and make its great Roman base depend upon a slender
Anglican apex, a method complimentary to both
Roman Catholicism and Anglicanism, according to the
way you look at the apex, which the Papist will regard
as an insignificant beginning to expanding truth and
the Anglican as the crown and perfection (which an
apex is by rights) spoiled by a monstrous excrescence.

Manning during his Cardinalate (1875–1892) was a noble, awe-inspiring figure, with passions which the Englishman could not fully understand, though they compelled his respect. He came into his own publicly by his masterly handling of the great Dockers' Strike led by Ben Tillett. He was deeply respected by Protestants for his rabid teetotalism. Even on the day he died (January 14, 1892) he refused to receive alcoholic stimulants, and no matter how ill he was he could be depended upon to attend a " Temperance " meeting, to speak in vile weather in the open air, or endure one stuffy meeting after another during holidays (invariably devoted to the Temperance crusade). It may be unbecoming in me to suggest that he was a fanatic in this respect when much of our present sobriety may be the result of his ardent zeal ; yet fanatic he was, apparently tinged with the Manichean heresy. He was a prolific writer whose influence was diminished by a didactic mode ; an eloquent preacher, with a rich style and honeyed and persuasive manner. To hear him was to be warmed, almost converted. Manning was the greatest barrister who has ever failed to appear at the Bar, even as Gladstone was the greatest Archbishop of Canterbury who has ever failed to enter the ministry. Roll all eminent barristers of the last few generations, such as Marshall Hall and Lord Birkenhead, into one, and you have Manning-the-might-have-been, who would have robbed the gallows of many a prisoner, innocent or otherwise. Roll all Archbishops of recent memory into one and you have Gladstone-the-might-have-been (though I do not, of course, suggest that Providence makes mistakes). Gladstone and Manning were school-chums, by the way, and life-long friends.

When gracing a banquet, at which he might have eaten a morsel—or not—for he lived a life of stern asceticism, his room at Westminster being a cell and his fare the simplest, he looked what he was, an ascetic who loved his fellow-beings too well to stand apart from them; when clothed in robes of office at a ceremony he might have been St. Augustine come down from a stained-glass window. There is no doubt that we should look upon him as a fine example of the saintly life, a view which may come somewhat as a shock to the younger generation of Anglo-Catholics (of whom I am one) whose affection for Newman has led them into a dislike for the memory of Manning.

He was a gentle friend to all who sought him, with a happy knack of making them feel that he understood their point of view entirely, and in a large measure sympathized with it. Like St. Paul, he could be all things to all men. For instance, he *really* admired the Salvation Army; he really appreciated the High Churchman who was not merely a ritualist; he really liked to join in learned discussions with atheists; and he really *loved* the poor and outcast and sinful.

I confess that I have disliked him on account of his treatment of Newman, but I confess, also, that he really believed, when he frustrated Newman's scheme to settle in Oxford to encourage Roman Catholic parents to send their boys there, that his liberalism suggested danger and an admission that education was not the primary concern of the Church. There was also the prosperity of the existing Catholic colleges to be considered.

He was a great administrator, with a martial disposition. As may be supposed, he was not always popular. Clergy established comfortably in well-to-do parishes, in which they had gained a notoriety for success, did not relish being told to pack their bags and go to some poverty-stricken district at a moment's notice. Nothing irks the lax more than such discipline. It is said that one of his own Canons once remarked that the death of Mrs. Manning was the greatest misfortune that had ever befallen the Catholic Church in England. But his sternness as an administrator was tempered by willingness to meet the disobedient face to face, and plead with them as father with sons. There is a pathetic story of how one of his elderly clergy refused to move from his comfortable cure, and remained excommunicate until, four years later, while he lay dying, the aged Cardinal came to plead with him and restore him to the Sacraments. He reminds me of the Apostle John in his love of the outcast. To build a great cathedral in London seemed to him idle until there were sufficient orphanages for the children whom he grieved to see torn from the bosom of the Church to be nurtured at the sterile breasts of Protestant Boards of Guardians.

Such I conceive to be Manning-of-the-purple. It is time to see Manning-of-the-Anglican-surplice; to turn from the great base to the slender apex.

He was born at Copped Hall, Totteridge, in Hertfordshire, on July 15, 1808. The house had been bought by his grandfather, a West India merchant. Manning's father followed a like avocation, taking a part, as well, in public affairs, by holding seats in Parliament for thirty years. He married twice, first the daughter of a banker, and then a lady, Mary Hunter, who came of an Italian family named Venatore. In his Italian blood may lie the explanation of Manning's " painless " transition to Romanism. Manning passed his boyhood at a school where Charles and Christopher Wordsworth were being educated.

With these boyish companions [says Hutton in his memoir], who were later to become bishops, of St. Andrew's and of Lincoln respectively, the youthful Manning had what is popularly called " a good time." Of the three he seems to have been the most venturesome and mischievous ; but a story that he told with some humour of an exploit in which they were all engaged—a raid on the vinery at Coombe Bank—puts the three future prelates pretty much on a level in this respect. His boyhood was distinguished from that of others who have subsequently become known as great ecclesiastics, in that he was a thorough boy, fond of games and of sport ; riding, shooting, boating and cricket being his especial favourites. As an old man he would still tell, with a gleam of satisfaction in his eye, that he killed a hare with his first shot.

A certain precocious dignity earned him the sobriquet of General. He went up to Balliol in 1827, and became noticeable for his persuasive oratorical powers. Then financial losses which his father had incurred cast their shadow upon him, and changed his life. He was thrown upon his own resources, and became transformed into a thoughtful scholar, gaining a much-needed first-class in his finals. He was converted by the discipline of disappointment and anxiety, the need of withdrawing into a shell in order to bring his studies to a successful end, and the frustration of his ambitious hopes of becoming a Parliamentary orator. At this time, too, he came under the influence of a good woman who afterwards wrote little books of piety. *Peep of Day* and *Line upon Line* provoke, I admit, one's risible faculties, and yet how ungenerous one is ! I perhaps owe more to them than I care to admit, or know how to admit ; and Manning was converted by their authoress. In a letter to *The Times* in 1892 it was pointed out that Miss Bevan, with whom he stayed at Trent Park, tried to cheer him,

telling him there were higher aims still that he had not thought of. " What are they ? " he asked. She replied, " The kingdom of heaven ; heavenly ambitions are not closed against you." He listened, and said in reply, he did not know but that she was right. She suggested reading the Bible together, saying she was sure her brother Robert (his school-chum, and later the well-known banker) would join them. This they did during the whole of that vacation, every morning after breakfast. It was her conviction that this was the beginning of Manning's religious life. He always used to speak of her as his spiritual mother.

To me it is a consoling thought that the future Cardinal Archbishop of Westminster was thus spiritually awakened by a pious evangelical lady. My happiness would be complete had he become Pope. From *Line upon Line* to the Throne of Peter would satisfy the most voracious appetite for sheer, unimaginable romance, and be a symbol of the inner unity of all forms of Christianity !

When he left Oxford he worked for a few months in the Colonial Office, but went back to prepare for Holy Orders, became a Fellow of Merton in 1832, and a year later Rector of Lavington with Graffham, near Chichester. He married, becoming brother-in-law to Samuel Wilberforce, afterwards Bishop of Oxford and Winchester. His wife was young and beautiful, but died childless four years later. Manning worshipped her, and his lovely Rectory, when she was gone, became a lonely retreat, for, holding strict Church principles, he would not marry again. He began to lose his life among his agricultural labourers, whose deplorable lot caused him constant worry. He took little or no part in the Oxford Movement, being a High Churchman of the old school and no more. But he read the Tracts and was influenced by them. What seized hold of his mind more than anything else was the need—the essential need—of unity in ecclesiastical organization. His oratorical genius seems, in the springtide of his Anglican ministry, to have flowered to the full, in a way which makes his later sermons seem but the luscious, over-ripe fruit of late summer. Here are examples of early oratory:

We have a people straitened by poverty—worn down by toil they labour from the rising to the setting of the sun; and the human spirit will faint or break at last. It is to this unrelenting round of labour that the sourness, so unnatural to our English poor, but now too often seen, is to be ascribed. There is something in humanity which pines for a season of brighter and fresher thoughts, and becomes sharp and bitter if it be not satisfied. . . . Time must be redeemed for the poor man. The world is too hard upon him, and makes him pay too heavy a toll out of his short life. . . . Little is needed to make their holiday. The green fields, and tools idle for a day, the church bells, an active game, simple fare, the sport of their children, the kindly presence and patient ear of superiors, is enough to make a village festival.

There is a passage worthy of Newman; but I am not so sure about the following, which should, however, delight the soul of James Douglas, of the *Daily Express*. It is a passage from a sermon about fallen women, preached in 1844 on behalf of the Magdalen Hospital, six years before his secession:

None are to be pitied more; none are more sinned against. Shame, fear and horror bar their return. The drop has fallen; behind them is a gulf they cannot pass. . . . God alone is witness of the groanings which are breathed unknown, and the burning tears which are shed in the very depths of impurity. What harrowing recollections of faces dearly loved, last seen in anguish, of the fresh years of early childhood, and the hopes and joys and fair prospects of an innocent and gentle life all seared and blasted, come back upon them in the hours of unholy revel, to be their mockery and torment. No eye but His can read the visions of home and happy days which rise upon their desolate hearts in the tumult and darkness of these crowded streets, and the agonizing dreams of a blessedness no longer theirs, by which their broken sleep is haunted. None other but He can know what unutterable agony goes up by day and by night from the loathsome chambers and pestilential dens in which these homeless, hopeless, decaying mortals hide themselves in misery to die. And what a death is the death of a harlot ! When the baffled heart wanders in dreams of sickness to die in the home of its birth, and waken up from the happiness of delirium to madden itself again in the sights and sounds which harass its miserable death-bed ; when the eye strains itself in vain for the vision of a mother's pitying face, and the ear is sick for the listening for the coming of brother, husband, child, whose footfall shall never be heard again. Then comes death, and after death the judgment, and the great white throne on which He sitteth from whose face both heaven and earth shall flee away. Lamb of God, that takest away the sin of the world, have mercy upon them and upon us in that day.

When Manning was made Archdeacon he quickly showed that he did not regard his office as an honorific sinecure. He visited every parish like a bishop, and issued charges regularly. From 1841 until his secession he grew to be a power in the diocese hardly second to the Bishop. His influence extended, indeed, far beyond it, and he came to be regarded as the virtual leader of the Oxford Revival, although he had had no hand in its inception. His power was greater than Pusey's or Keble's, and increased with the loss of Newman. Men's eyes were upon him as one marching straight to Canterbury, and fair might have been the pilgrimage of Anglo-Catholics down a century had he sat in the seat of Augustine. He had a way of overcoming opposition such as none possessed in equal measure. He had become a thorough Catholic without ever having worn a chasuble or kindled incense at the altar. He had a passion for unity which would have led him, as Primate, in spite of his prejudice against Romanism (which made Newman once to refuse to see him), to anticipate Malines by several decades. He would have made his presence *felt*, and the House of Lords, had he been there when it played shuttlecock and battledore with the revised Prayer Book, would have been overwhelmed by his influence, as the Commons would have writhed under his censure. Indeed, there is nothing that might not have happened. But it was not to be.

The Gorham Judgment is a humiliating episode of English Church history, inexcusably disgraceful. A Mr. Gorham, a minister with Calvinistic sympathies, held that grace was not necessarily given before Holy Baptism, in it or after it. The Bishop of Exeter refused to institute him to a benefice. The Lord

Chancellor, who had presented Mr. Gorham with the living, opposed the Bishop. The Court of Arches upheld the Bishop, but the Judicial Committee of the Privy Council reversed its decision. That Committee, which had no true ecclesiastical character, was composed of Sumner, Archbishop of Canterbury; Musgrave, Archbishop of York; Blomfield, Bishop of London, and six laymen. Its preposterous claim to be the final authority in matters of faith disturbed Manning terribly, and in 1851 England was shocked by his secession. Within a few weeks, to the indignation of old Roman Catholics, he was " re-ordained " a priest, to return some years later to found the Congregation of the Oblates of St. Charles at Bayswater. By this time he was the friend and confidant of Pope Pius IX, who made him Archbishop of Westminster in 1865 and Cardinal ten years later.

He was an ardent supporter of the temporal power of the Pope, an ultramontane of ultramontanes. The convening of the Vatican Council to define the dogma of Infallibility was as welcome to him as it was painful to Newman, who seemed to regard as a personal affront, complaining bitterly, while forgetting the definition of the dogma of the Immaculate Conception, that Œcumenical Councils were never convened unless the Faith was impugned.

A Council's proper office is [Newman maintained] when some great heresy or other evil impends, to inspire hope and confidence in the faithful, but now . . . we are told to prepare for something, we know not what, to try our faith, we know not how! No impending danger is to be averted, but a great difficulty is to be created! Is this the proper work of an Œcumenical Council? What have we done to be treated as the faithful never were treated before? When has a definition *de fide* been a luxury of devotion and not a stern painful necessity?

The rustic quietude of Sussex; the peaceful hills on which sheep graze away unthinking lives; the murmurous streams that thread sinuous, silvery ribands through the woodlands; lose sweet serenity when a storm breaks over them. The men of Lavington are used to storms. They bring in their oxen from the ploughing and drive their sheep into the folds. A storm means an extra hour of leisure, a pleasant wind-fall, if none of their beasts has strayed. They take off their wet smocks then, and wash, and put on their Sunday ones, and brave the rain to the tavern, or sit around the fireside with their bairns until it is time to betake themselves to their beds, where, for a few hours only, they can forget their troubles. One trouble never ceases to fret their minds; an incomprehensible trouble, one that has robbed them of the priest they loved and trusted. *Their* Mr. Manning has joined the Pope of Rome. A cruel blow, the Pope being a wicked creature condemned in the Revelations. He is up in "Lunnon," now, in a palace, dressed in scarlet when he should be striding over the fields to ring his bell for daily service. Ah! he wore proper black then. The years wear on, and

these downsmen cease not to revere his memory.
Why, he baptized many of them, and cared for them
in their childhood, and led them to the Sacrament.
And now he is a Cardinal, and so far gone in Popery
that they can never hope for his return, and " some
do say that he may be Pope o' Rome hisself before
he's finished, and repented."

A storm in the heavens they understand. It is
nature. A storm in a Church is a storm in a tea-cup.
It seems to be about nothing. Yet it lasted until the
last of them slept with his fathers, perhaps recalling
wistfully on his death-bed, with simple, faithful love,
how the Archdeacon had patted his head one morning
when he met him going out for mushrooms, and bade
him say his prayers in the church when returning.
When the decree affirming Infallibility was passed a
terrific storm of thunder and lightning broke over
Rome. Manning may have thought of Sussex. Did
he think, in the midst of successful and engrossing
labours, of the suffering of his yokels ? One wonders.
" Ah, sir ! " said one of the rustics once to Manning's
successor at Lavington, pointing to the setting sun,
" that is just what the Archdeacon was so fond of. He
used often to admire it, as he stood, over the
hill there : ' Don't it look beautiful, John, sinking
to rest when his work is done? That is how you
and I will sink to rest when our work is done, if ' "—
here the old man's memory failed him—" ' *if we has
luck.*' "

The bell still peals over Lavington, for men may

come and men may go, but *Ecclesia Anglicana* survives the storms of winter by God's Providence, and goes on in the freshness of a second spring, for all her fresh springs are in Zion.

XI

CHRISTINA ROSSETTI

1830–1894

CHRISTINA ROSSETTI was born on December 5, 1830, in Charlotte Street, Portland Place, London, the youngest child of Gabriel Rossetti, an Italian poet who had taken refuge in this country from political enemies. His wife was Frances Polidori, whose brother had been Byron's companion and physician abroad.

Christina's brothers and sisters became famous, but none more so than Dante Gabriel, one of the founders of the Pre-Raphaelite school, whose paintings " Beata Beatrix " and the " Annunciation " are in the National Gallery. Christina was his model for the latter, for she was beautiful, though she wore ugly clothes and thick shoes.

Although of Italian origin, the children were brought up in the tenets of the Anglican Church. One of them, Maria Francesca, forsook authorship to become an All Saints' Sister. Christina herself shines next to Keble in the poetical constellation of Anglo-Catholicism.

She was educated at home by her mother. Miss Proctor says :

As the constant companion of her brothers, it may not be wrong to say that she acquired an independence of thought and feeling which, with an ordinary English education, she could scarcely have attained. Hers was a delightfully happy home : love, poetry, art, religion— everything that could make life sweet.

The children read the same books, learned Italian perfectly, and were strongly influenced by their father. Christina could read the operatic poems of Metastasio in Italian when but ten years old, and was deeply versed in Shakespeare, Scott, Byron and Burns. Her first poem was written in 1842 when she was eleven. Thus :

TO MY MOTHER

To-day's your natal day,
    Sweet flowers I bring ;
Mother, accept, I pray,
    My offering.

And may you happy live,
    And long us bless ;
Receiving as you give
    Great happiness.

Her grandfather Polidori printed her youthful poems privately.

When she was nineteen she became a contributor (as Ellen Alleyne) to a short-lived magazine called *The Germ*, or *Thoughts towards Nature in Poetry, Literature, and Art*. Some of her finest poems appeared therein, among them " Dream Land." Hard times had come. Her father's sight was failing. Christina taught in a little school which her mother conducted in Camden Town and later at Frome.

Her sweetness of character was ennobled by frustration. She had two *affaires du cœur*. When seventeen she fell in love with a foolish youth named James Collinson. He became a Papist, and she would not follow him. He entered a Jesuit seminary, but on being required to clean boots as an act of humility returned to indifferent painting. Her second love was Charles Cayley, but religious scruples intervened again. This was a tragedy. William Rossetti says: " No woman ever loved a man more deeply, or more constantly." Most women would have become embittered or austere, but her devotion to God touched every sombre cloud with light.

Her poetical powers won full recognition in 1862 with " Goblin Market." By the age of thirty-five she reached her zenith, and was revealed to the public as a spiritual genius. Consider the majesty of her poem on Heaven :

Multitudes, multitudes stood up in bliss,
   Made equal to the angels, glorious, fair ;
With harps, palms, wedding garments, kiss of peace,
   And crowned and haloed hair.

.   .   .   .   .

Glory touched glory on each blessèd head,
   Hands locked dear hands never to sunder more ;
These were the new-begotten from the dead
   Whom the great birthday bore.

She was a member of Christ Church, Albany Street,

and her spiritual adviser was Dr. Littledale, a " free lance " priest of singular genius, who contributed to many journals and figured in most of the controversies of the time. I could profitably devote a chapter to Dr. Littledale, but must suffice myself by indicating why Christina was drawn to him. He has been called the " Father of Ritualism," and he certainly nurtured the outward and visible form of the Oxford Movement.

He found [said a priest in a panegyric] Ritualism . . . in his study, in the university, in the library, in the drawing-room ; and he brought it out into the streets and lanes. He found it among scholars, antiquaries, and *dilettanti* ; he vulgarized it, in the true sense of the word ; he gave it to the common crowd ; he found reasons and justification for those who used it.

But what he did for its outward form he did also for its soul. His witty versatility rescued Ritualism from the hands of archæologists and gentlemen.

With his large, earnest brown, though deeply sunken, eyes, and long, grey beard sweeping over his breast, he (seemed like) some benevolent and learned monk of the third or fourth century in the midst of an Alexandrian library ; and his chambers, full of ecclesiastical ornaments, and resembling the abode of a recluse, heightened this impression. . . . He was an excellent talker, and his humour was intensified by a perceptible brogue.

He suffered much physical pain, but it seemed only to stimulate him to constant labour. He was a true journalist, because he could write at a moment's notice on any subject under the sun, but he wrote with *knowledge.* Beatrice Rosenthal considers that his keen sense of humour and cheerful outlook on life must have exercised a wholesome influence on Christina, " with her strain of morbidity due to ill-health."

Her later life was spent in London (which she loathed) waiting upon an invalid aunt with unfailing cheerfulness, dreaming the while of leafy lanes, and green meadows, and mossy woods splashed with primroses. " Not on any account," she said once, " would I leave my aunt for a day, even. One day, perhaps, when I am alone, I shall see the country again." And yet she wrote :

> Why, one day in the country
> Is worth a month in town ;
> Is worth a day and a year.

" As I no longer go to the country from time to time," she wrote to Miss Proctor, " I may say that the country very graciously comes to me, for friends send or bring me flowers." Her passionate love of the country appears in many of her poems and letters. London affected her in another way, reminding us of how we have failed, since her day, to solve the problem of the " down and out." She was wounded to think of the suffering of the destitute and wrote : " The contrast between London luxury and London destitution is really appalling. All sorts of gaieties advertised, and deaths by exposure or starvation recorded in the same newspaper."

Soon after her aunt died she became ill, and could

not enjoy her freedom. Her beloved flowers consoled her. "Thank you," she wrote, "for flowers, which bring a country charm and freshness to our world of brick and mortar. Not that I despise the square trees, which are greening delightfully. Those wild blue hyacinths . . . have a special hold on me." On her last Easter she wrote: "Thank you for the pretty primroses and daisies in their envelope of moss . . ." "A box of primroses, etc., has come to-day, bringing something of the country to my little room; so I need not envy you your primroses! And now we are having thunder since I wrote that."

Beatrice Rosenthal says:

She died at her house in Torrington Square, after a painful illness, on the Feast of St. Thomas of Canterbury, 1894, going out with the old year, whose dirge she sang in that wonderful poem, "Passing away, saith the world, passing away," with its reiterated rhyme that beats on the ear like midnight bells. She, whose life was marked by self-effacement, is best remembered by lines such as those, and by her matchless carol, "In the bleak mid-winter" —one of the loveliest things, surely, that ever came out of Bloomsbury.

She died in the calm spirit in which she had written:

> When flowers are yet in bud
>   While the boughs are green,
> I would get quit of earth,
>   And get robed for heaven;
> Putting on my raiment white within the screen,
> Putting on my crown of gold whose gems are seven.

Christina secured her meed of praise in her own day.

CHRISTINA ROSSETTI

The *Century Magazine* described her as the most perfect
of the contemporary poets. There is, indeed, form
and finish in her poems, and a poet's generation is not
necessarily purblind, even though it often exalts the
mediocre while deriding the work of genius. We
must not say that, because Christina Rossetti was
recognized in her day, therefore she was mediocre.
We may be poor judges of past work, as in the case of
Francis Thompson (still neglected) as well as of present, as in the case of Sir William Watson. But she is
certainly spoiled by quantity, and an incapacity to
select and eliminate. Her poems have an inimitable,
individual character, and open doors into the supernatural; touching Heaven like rainbows. Here
is my favourite (with acknowledgments to the
S.P.C.K.) :

> Thy lovely Saints do bring Thee love,
> >   Incense and joy and gold :
> Fair star with star, fair dove with dove,
> >   Beloved by Thee of old.
> I, Master, neither star nor dove,
> >   Do bring my sins and tears ;
> Yet I, too, bring a little love,
> >   Amid my flaws and fears.
> A trembling love that faints and fails,
> >   And yet is love of thee.
> A wondering love that hopes and hails,
> >   Thy wondrous love for me.
> Love kindling faith and pure desire,
> >   Love following on to bliss.
> A spark, O Jesu, from Thy fire,
> >   A drop from Thine abyss.

XII

CHARLES FUGE LOWDER

1820–1880

ON the ninth of September, in the year of grace 1930, in the æon of motor-cars and airplanes, and other detestable enormities of civilization which make men forget the fathers that begat them, by the commotion they create, an inquiring journalist, disengaged from scooping up a crime yarn (if one dare suggest so unlikely a contingency), might, had he been by chance in the churchyard of Chislehurst (an even more unlikely event, as it was pouring with rain), have seen no fewer than two hundred persons grouped in homage around a grave half a century old.

He would have sought a clue from the grave. " Charles Fuge Lowder," he would have said ; " now who was he, and why the fuss and commotion ? " Then, gathering a story from the circumstances of the day (the rain being stressed) and the lips of some of the pilgrims, he would, in the manner of journalists, have missed the point completely.

I am a journalist as well as an author. I do not know the difference between a journalist and an author, any more than I know the difference between a painter of miniatures and one who paints on canvas (if there is a difference), but I know what I should have done. I should have taken the first train to wherever the remains of C. J. Blomfield, Lord Bishop of London in the fifties of the last century, lay, forgotten by the world, and drawn from the contrast a story which would have cheered the hearts of the boys of Britain, and made them love the clergy.

Permit me to present it.

The famous church of St. Barnabas, Pimlico, was, in the fifties, the scene of riotings, and, when the fightings without were ended, fears within ensued. St. Barnabas was a daughter church of St. Paul's, Knightsbridge, and one of the candidates for the office of churchwarden at the latter was a Mr. Westerton, a bigoted Protestant, who had been no end of a trouble. St. Barnabas possessed an underground passage from the choirboys' vestry to the crypt, and, as may be imagined, underground passages and choirboys combined are sources of trouble. In the passage there lurked, one day, a group of keen young choristers, their leader being a Christ's Hospital boy who was a cousin of the clergyman whose grave we have been considering. He was a very angry boy at that moment, because he had seen a man in Ebury Street carrying sandwich-boards inscribed with *Vote for Westerton !* and something had to be done about it. In the midst of the argument the Rev. Charles Fuge Lowder, a young man of pious demeanour, whose record was exemplary, came upon the scene. The boy entreated his cousin to allow them to pelt the sandwich-man, whose only offence, had they considered the matter with as much eagerness for charity as for Catholicism (but there were riots in those days, and pelting was as familiar to suffering Catholics as *Amens*), was an effort to earn a dinner, and received an astonishing permission. Charles Fuge Lowder gave them sixpence to buy rotten eggs, but bade them use no stones nor dirt. With a whoop of delight they equipped themselves with political missiles, and drove the wretched man off his beat. He went to his employers, and they to the magistrate, and Charles Fuge Lowder, who gallantly took all the blame, found himself in dock. He apologized publicly, and the case was dismissed, but more trouble was brewing. The newspapers made capital out of the story, proclaiming a Puseyite conspiracy, and an ominous note arrived from the Bishop of London, thus :

The Bishop of London requests the Rev. C. F. Lowder to call at London House to-morrow, at half-past ten o'clock.
May 3, 1854.

The outcome was not a revocation of his licence, as he had feared, but suspension from the exercise of his functions, as Curate of St. Barnabas, for six weeks. Shortly afterwards a crestfallen young clergyman might have been seen embarking for the Continent for his holiday, fortunate to have lived in the last century, rather than the era of illustrated papers. Thus ended the incident which the Bishop afterwards alluded to as " Lowder's ovation." The Bishop was harsh in suspending him, for publicity had been pain enough. Where are the pilgrims to Bishop Blomfield's tomb, and why are there pilgrims to Lowder's ?

The incident of the " ovation " was curious in view of Charles Lowder's earnest piety, and experience, and stiffness of character. He saw the light of day at Bath on June 22, 1820 (the first-born of very pious parents), his father being a partner in the Old Bath Bank, which foundered, completely altering the family circumstances, which had, throughout Charles's childhood, been affluent. Charles had a keen desire to become a missionary, and evolved various schemes to fulfil it and at the same time support his family. They came to nothing. He was ever a leader, as a sturdy boy, and at King's and at Exeter College, Oxford. One or two uneventful curacies preceded his work in Pimlico, and then, the pelting episode forgiven if not forgotten, with Catholic sympathies enlarged by visits to the Continent (on which he was passionately keen), came his great chance. He had helped to found a brotherhood for priests, of a secret kind, called the Society of the Holy Cross, which wished to institute a mission in Dockland. It was welcomed generously by the Rev. Bryan King, rector of St. George's-in-the-East, whose parish contained

733 houses, of which 40 were gin palaces and 145 brothels. The terrible Ratcliff Highway was part of the parish and Bryan King, who had worked heroically for fifteen years, was glad to be assisted by Lowder and companion missioners, who ultimately lived together. The correspondence between Lowder and Bryan King which led to the inauguration of the mission reveal the former as of imperious and pernickety disposition, and the latter as a very perfect and patient gentleman, seeking only the good of the Church and the maintenance of ecclesiastical principles. Lowder would write long and tedious letters, demanding one concession after another, and Bryan King would reply with gentleness, giving way on personal matters and being firm on ecclesiastical. The correspondence is a revelation of how an elderly priest should deal with a young one. Yet such a man, though he may engender dislike among his equals, is ideally fitted for warfare with brothel-keepers.

Lowder's work had been patiently carried on for some years when the riots broke out. He had now the magnificent Mackonochie (afterwards of St. Alban's, Holborn) as one of his helpers. Mackonochie's coming brought about a revival. During the riots the Mission chapels were invaded and the Mission house was attacked. Lowder and Mackonochie were required by Bishop Blomfield to officiate at the parish church, and were thus exposed to the rioters.

An eyewitness writes :

CHARLES FUGE LOWDER

I don't know that on any occasion Mr. Lowder lost his equanimity. He was summoned before the magistrate and fined for shutting the vestry door of the parish church upon a man who, having no right to be there, insisted upon trying to force his way in ; but he made no comment upon this beyond mentioning the fact, which he did with a smile, at the incongruity of his being fined for protecting God's house, while it seemed impossible to get anyone punished for desecrating it.

In any other part of London I do not think that these riots would have been tolerated for a month, but St. George's-in-the-East is removed from the quiet thoroughfares of the metropolis ; violence and disorder were chronic there, and months were allowed to pass before the authorities showed themselves to be in earnest in putting them down. . . .

. . . One of the most conspicuous of [the rioters] (I believe that he was the original " aggrieved parishioner ") was fined at the Middlesex Sessions for keeping houses of ill-fame, and the rest were not famous for their purity or their piety.

The character of some of these men was thus set forth by a young man who attended the night school in the Calvert Street district : " It's all a question of beer, sir, and what else they can get. We know them. They are blackguards like ourselves here. Religion ain't anything more to them than it is to us. They gets paid for what they do, and they do it like they'd do any other job."

The Bishop of London, Dr. Blomfield, sent no word of sympathy, as the riots went on Sunday after Sunday for a year, but rather reproached the clergy for not making terms with the mob for the sake of peace. They were brought to an end only by the

133

resignation of Bryan King. We need to study the Catholic movement in its early parochial phases if we would face with courageous equanimity the riots that occur in these days, for the Movement seems to be back where it was, and a new note of hostility is evident where for a quarter of a century there has been toleration.

Lowder's patient work was rewarded in 1866 by the consecration of the permanent church of St. Peter's, London Docks. His had been an uphill task for ten years. He possessed no gift of eloquence, and often preached over his people's heads. He had become a rather stern, aloof priest, indefatigable in his routine, and not well understood even by fellow-clergy, whose lives he ordered under an uncomfortable and Spartan *régime*. I imagine him to have been a thoroughgoing autocrat, not untainted by that foul disease known among curates as " vicaritis," a pestilence which comes upon curates themselves with seeming inevitability as soon as they are elevated to the dignity of incumbency. His head was bald. His prayers were many. If his will was as iron, his heart was of gold. His title was " Mister " in the neighbourhood. It was to be changed to " Father " almost as soon as the bells of St. Peter's had finished chiming for the consecration.

Cholera is far worse than bubonic plague and the black death. It suddenly came upon Wapping. Men and women and children succumbed to it. On every hand there was weeping and woe. Father

Lowder became the hero of the parish. No priest could have murmured the Compline psalm in a more literal sense than he, as he went about, hour after hour, day after day, ministering in fœtid rooms to the sick and dying, smoothing the bundles that served the poor for pillows, wrapping little plague-stricken whimpering children in blankets and carrying them in his arms to hospital, appealing to the outside world for funds for necessities (and securing them, thanks to *The Times*), shriving, communicating, burying, in peril of his life. Let the words be his epitaph who was not afraid for any terror by night : nor for the arrow that flieth by day : for the pestilence that walketh in darkness : nor for the sickness that destroyeth in the noonday. A thousand fell beside him and ten thousand at his right hand, but it came not nigh him. God had given His angels charge over him, to keep him in all his ways.

When the scourge went he was *Father* Lowder. The people had seen through him at last, and found a saint. Though their ways lay in the vale of darkness still, and selfishness and bestiality and incest and thievery raised evil heads to leer at the Cross and those who upheld it, the battle was won. The Church—and the Church meant Father Lowder—could never again be ignored.

Hundreds of souls have been saved, and the children of Wapping, grown up and married, with tots of their own at St. Peter's, have learnt to look upon the Father as one of the few permanencies in their life of chance and change.

Then came a day when the unthinkable happened. Lowder was abroad, seeing the Passion Play at Oberammergau. Then he was at Zell-am-See, and ill. Then came news of his death, on September 9, 1880. Miss Trench says, in her biography :

> They said who knew the truth, that when the tidings from Zell-am-See reached St. Peter's and spread through court and alley, there were stricken hearts in homes so poor and wretched that they might be thought beyond the sympathies of life, crouching over the few embers of the grate, too crushed to speak, almost too crushed to think, but trying in a dazed way to take in the meaning of the terrible words : " Father Lowder is dead."

The church of St. Peter's has been full since dawn, hundreds of people awaiting the coming of the bier, communicating at the first celebration at 3. " It was the most solemn night I ever saw," said a witness. " The crowds of people in the street that night waiting for news : all poor people, with blanched faces, and the sorrow of their hearts speaking through their eyes ; so quiet and resigned, and not murmuring . . . ; just hanging about in groups as people do when struck down by a common sorrow." Then tidings came of the coffin, which had been delayed in its journey from Zell-am-See. At last it came,

passing [as the writer of Father Lowder's biography says] up the lane through the crowds of weeping people to the dock-bridge, which bounds the parish. Once, during the St. George's riots, his friends had made a line across this bridge, and held it against the mob who had hunted him down, threatening to throw him into the docks ; and now, in the streets where he had been pelted and ill-treated, the police were obliged to keep a line amidst the crowds of weeping men who pressed forward to see and touch the pall beneath which their benefactor slept.

The church was crammed, and thousands stood outside, many of them setting off on foot to the churchyard of Chislehurst. When the coffin at length reached Chislehurst Common there were three thousand men of Wapping to welcome it.

My essay ends where it began, though half a century earlier.

The sun was just setting, at the close of a lovely day, as the coffin, covered with flowers, was lowered into the moss-lined grave, the choirs singing, " Brother, now thy toils are over." Slowly and tearfully the multitude of men, women, and children passed round . . . to take a last look at the resting-place of him they loved. No such funeral, it was truly said, has been seen in England in modern tir .s. Thanksgiving and the voice of melody in the streets of East London on a working-day, the whole populace turning out, the church adorned in white and beautiful with flowers—all symbolized, not the sorrow of those without hope, but the last and best genuine earthly reward of a good man. But of all grand points in that funeral, certainly the most beautiful and touching was the little children, fringing the crowd, and weeping as if their hearts would break. . . . And they who loved him best, remembering the bright promise of his boyhood and youth, and the worn weary face of later years, could not mourn that the patient, faithful soldier should now wear the crown, and hear his Master's gracious call: " Enter thou into the joy of thy Lord."

I have not been able to find an account of Bishop Blomfield's burial.

XIII

ROBERT RADCLYFFE DOLLING
1851–1902

ROBERT RADCLYFFE DOLLING was a judgment both upon the Anglican Communion and them who worked deeds of darkness. The latter retreated in disorder before him. The former drove him from an apostolic work, unwanted. . . . "I am come to send fire on the earth." Dolling was fire.

The fire was wholly spiritual, and a few understood it. But the moderate Bishop Walsham How, who penned these gracious lines, knew what manner of man he was:

At morn he fed his soul with angels' food
Holding with Heaven high mystic communing,
That from the mount some radiance he might bring
Down to the weary earth-bound multitude.
At night among the restless throng he stood,
Sharer of all their mirth and revels gay,
Yet holding over all a watchful sway,
And tempering every rude ungracious mood.
Not in cheap words he owned mankind his kin ;
For them his life, his all, he yearned to spend,
That he their love and trust might wholly win,
And all their rough ways to his moulding bend,
Shielding them from the unholy grasp of sin,
And owned by them a brother and a friend.

The Dolling sisters were more remarkable than their brother. His bishop, he has told us in *Ten Years in a Portsmouth Slum* (a book which social workers and clergy should study), evinced considerable nervousness when he said that he would bring his sisters to Landport. " He suggested that their dress might frighten the people. I said I hoped it would not. He intimated other difficulties. But his face brightened up considerably, when I told him that they were fleshly and not religious sisters. . . ."

These gentle women had fearful odds to contend with. They had to live in shocking quarters. They were frail, and seemingly too gentle to deal with rough girls. And the rough girls were wild to a degree. With fearless persistence, however, they laboured at Landport for ten years, seeking for wandering girls in brothels, despite the malevolence of those who made a living by wrecking souls and bodies ; sharing the troubles of poor and destitute mothers ; caring for, and often taking out of evil environment, little girls ; praying ; teaching ; living lives of such saintly sweetness that in time the character of those to whom they ministered was wholly changed. And this in no spirit of puritanism, for one of the first steps they took was to inaugurate dances and bring the wild lads and lassies together. No doubt the work was the fulfilment of their hearts' desire, but, like all who do works of splendour, they could not realize the sunshine they shed upon those who lived in the shadows. They saw their daily failures vividly. The heaviness that endures in the night-time must assuredly have overcome them every morning but for two factors, one heavenly, one human. The heavenly was Grace, the human nationality.

Robert Radclyffe Dolling was born in Magheralin, County Down, on February 10, 1851. His father was a landed proprietor, at one time High Sheriff of Londonderry, but English. His mother, a niece of the first Earl of Caledon, was Irish.

He was a deeply religious child, much interested in theology, although when a student at Salisbury he was to set up a record for theological inefficiency by spending most of his time in mission work instead of in the lecture room. His theology was of a rather concrete sort. At the age of four he said at dinner, to a guest who had expressed some difficulty over the dogma of the Holy Trinity :

" I've got meat and potatoes and gravy on my plate. That's three things. But it's only one dinner. That's like the Trinity."

He was a lovable, unselfish boy, never a prig ; and early developed a passion for helping others. Thus we find him in young manhood conducting classes and clubs for the Irish boys. Journeys to England on his father's business gave him an opportunity to do slum work, under the direction of Father Stanton of St. Alban's, Holborn. They called Dolling " Brother Bob."

After his father's death he decided to seek ordination. He was a problem to the college authorities, and had little in common with his fellow-students. He was thankful to get away from the studious atmosphere to the " real work," but in after life regretted lost opportunities, and tried to make amends by reading theology for an hour every day.

He was placed in charge of a mission at Mile End, where he did a magnificent work for two years, throwing it up impetuously because he could not have a free hand. Mile End's loss was Landport's gain.

Landport, he says, had very narrow and quaint streets named after admirals and sea-battles, with old-world, red-tiled roofs, and interiors like cabins.

Many times I have stuck in a staircase, and could not go up or down till pulled from below . . . the far-off scent of the sea coming over the mud of the harbour, and every now and then the boom of a cannon, or the shrill shriek of the siren ; sailors everywhere, sometimes fighting, sometimes courting, nearly always laughing and good-humoured. . . . I remember well how, the first night I made acquaintance with it, their uniforms and rolling gait redeemed from its squalor and commonplace this poor district, with its eleven hundred little houses and its fifty-two public-houses. Charlotte Street was, from end to end, an open fair ; cheap jacks screaming ; laughing crowds round them ; never seeming to buy ; women, straggling under the weight of a baby, trying to get the Sunday dinner a little cheaper because things had begun to get stale ; great louts of lads standing at the corners—you can guess from their faces the kind of stories they are telling; then some piece of horse-play . . . slatternly women creeping out of some little public-house. . . . I think if I had paid this visit before I accepted the Mission, I should never have accepted it. The shrill gaiety was a revelation to me of utter hopelessness, such as I had never imagined before.

And yet he knew from childhood the poverty of the Irish peasant, and from early manhood the slums of Holborn. Landport a revelation! Landport must have been *awful* . . .

He began work in a mood of hopelessness. The children had been described as a " savage crew," and were, to his horror, old in knowledge. Prostitution was a normal feature of the drab existence of their elders in many cases, and rough louts came to jeer and swear into the church.

On my first Sunday afternoon [he says], as I was walking in Chance Street, I saw, for the first time, a Landport dance. Two girls, their only clothing a pair of sailors' trousers each, and two sailor lads, their only clothing the girls' petticoats, were dancing a kind of breakdown up and down the street, all the neighbours looking on amused but unastonished, until one couple, the worse for drink, toppled over. I stepped forward to help them up, but my endeavour was evidently looked upon from a hostile point of view, for the parish voice was translated into a shower of stones, until the unfallen sailor cried out, " Don't touch the Holy Joe. He doesn't look such a bad sort." I could not stay to cement our friendship, for the bell was ringing for children's service, and, to my horror, I found that some of the children in going to church had witnessed the whole of this scene.

143

They evidently looked upon it as quite a legitimate Sunday afternoon's entertainment. One little girl, of about eight, volunteered the name of the two dancing girls; she was a kind of little servant in the house, though she slept two or three doors off, and her only dread was that the return of a sailor, who had more rights in the house, might take place before the others had been got rid of.

But in time he found his feet, and, little by little, provided the remedies needed: a derelict chapel for a gymnasium; a home in the country for little orphan girls; organizations for men and women; a Church Brigade for boys. Father Dolling had a way that extracted money from the tightest purse. His "money grubbing," as he called it, resulted, during ten years, in a little over £50,000, every penny being won by strenuous effort, by preaching and lecturing and writing, especially by praying. This part of his work must have been a terrible drain on his strength, for he often embarked upon expensive ventures of faith without the wherewithal, trusting God and his friends to pull him through, and they did so. But the strongest faith in Providence cannot wholly quieten anxiety, and there must have come upon even such a valiant heart as his the distress and darkness that follows upon courageous plunges criticized by foes and friends. I can well understand his daily agony, for behind me lie years of begging, and years more are in store. I suspect that the collapse of his work in the end, under episcopal displeasure, may be traced as much to weariness as to impetuosity. Besides a magnificent church, he founded schools, maintained a penitentiary, financed emigration, and built a parsonage (sorely needed after the wretched quarters he had been condemned to live in during the early years). His charities were only limited by his departure, and his open House was like nothing on earth.

There foregathered, day in, year out, the desolate and the drunkard, the unemployed and the sailor lad, the ex-convict and the fallen parson, in one astonishing family, breaking their bread at one table. I do not pretend to understand how he kept it up.

> I shall never forget [he writes] the look on the face of Dr. Thorold one morning when I told him that the two companions he had chosen to sit with at supper the night before were both experienced thieves. One had been in gaol three times, the other twice; the former, a clergyman's son. . . . We generally sat at meals according to the order of our coming, but I thought he, being a Bishop, and unaccustomed to our ways, had better choose his own companions. I had only seen the lads the day before, and I watched the scene with amusement, qualified with terror for his ring and watch.

Like all clergy who hold a prominent place in the eye of the public, he was pestered by men who thought they had vocations for the ministry. One so pitied him in his ill-health that he got up a little collection for his benefit, but himself took a holiday with the proceeds. The discipline of laughter—and it was a merry household—and the discipline of labour soon choked these off. He says:

Once I remember a man almost prostrating himself at my feet, and saying, " All I crave is a habit." It was before I sold my library, and I saw that the books were very dusty, so getting a cloth I made him clean them, and then begin a catalogue. Before a week was over, tired of the catalogue, he had fled. Oh, most blessed catalogue, what a number of vocations it has discovered as non-existent !

Fallen and dissolute clergy vexed his righteous soul, and he had a particular horror of the ex-Roman.

Almost my first day in Portsmouth [he writes] I was persecuted by a wretched priest, whom, as soon as he had opened his mouth, I discovered to be a drunkard and a liar. He arrived one evening about five with a little bag in his hand. When I told him I was too busy to talk to him, he said, " I will leave my bag, and return at dinner-time." Then when I told him there was only one dinner for two, and neither I nor my secretary would share ours with him, he said, " Oh, it does not matter ; but I will return to sleep." And when I told him that there were but two bedrooms, and neither I nor my secretary would share these with him, the mask fell off his face. He had been received into the Church of England, and the Church of England was bound to support him ; he would soon make it too hot for me in Portsmouth. I never stood face to face with a more hideous blackmailer, but it was not until I had opened the door and had taken him by the back of the neck that he retired.

Sometimes, he confesses, the devil got loose and everything went wrong. Boys stole, men came in drunk, and there was insubordination. Dolling was a firm disciplinarian when aroused, and on one of these occasions condemned the household to bread and cheese for several days, instead of the usual good meal. Once he had a Christmas dinner carried away because Blind Willie had been tormented. Blind Willie had been a mudlark, searching in the filth of the harbour for pennies which nit-wits threw him. He had a wretched stepfather and a blind and paralysed mother who lay on some rags in a hovel. His two sisters, one older than him and one younger, earned sixpence a night without daring to reveal to the bed-ridden woman how it was come by. After his mother died he went blind, and having no one to care for him became one of Dolling's family, and organ-blower. He died in the imbecile ward of the Union, but had been a power for good in the strange household.

Dolling's love for children is revealed in another poignant story. " There is a little boy just come into Alfred Street," the district visitor said one day. " He is fourteen, but he looks like a child of five, and lives and sleeps in a little perambulator. There is no one to look after him, for his mother is in a lunatic asylum, and his father goes out at six in the morning, and does not come back till night."

" And so exactly I found him [says Dolling], our dear little Harry, all alone in this dark room in his perambulator, and on a little shelf, which his poor twisted hands could reach, his cold and wretched meals apportioned for the day. At first when we brought him to the house he was very timid and very nervous, but he soon brightened up . . . he was with us all day, and his little tender thread was soon woven into the woof of our common life, and on all our rough people his influence was as the influence of a little child. Sometimes, when all else fails, the roughest beasts are led by a little child. His face would wince with pain, when any boy spoke harshly to another. . . . I do not think I have ever seen such devotion to the Blessed Sacrament as in that little soul. In it he saw not only Jesus, but our Father, and even heaven as well. Strange, wonderful stories he told me of what he had seen there, for sometimes he would doze all day by the fire in the dining-room, in my study, or in Mary's kitchen, and then only say, "I was dreaming of the Blessed Sacrament. Do you think someone would wheel me to Mass to-morrow morning?" I remember so well kissing away the last tears I saw in his eyes, as he held up in his little shrunken hands some woollen slippers, which he had made for me, a little secret for my birthday, and found that there was not work enough done, and then fell back saying, "I shall never live to finish them," and died that night.

Such was the tender priest who could soundly box a server's ears for informing him, in holy horror, that he did not hold his fingers correctly at Mass, or a hooligan's for some act of devilment. It was tenderness mixed with firmness that made them worship him, and his study by day and his bedroom by night dominated the extraordinary household. His immense capacity for taking pains with the detail of parochial life (I do not mean the keeping of lists and registers and accounts and the mending of lace and linen and all the minutiæ that make an "efficient" church) shames one into wretchedness. Many souls live around one's church, year in and out, whom one knows by sight but never speaks to. He knew all his. Mother Church reached out through him and his sisters into a thousand dark corners. How I know not. I can but confess that, ardent as I was when, like Dolling, I commenced a ministry in the slums, I saw a little cripple boy who might have been a Harry, sitting in a chair on the pavement all day long. I must have seen him hundreds of times, but he seemed to shrink from me, and, save for a few words once or twice, I never broke through his reticence. I never got him to church. But Dolling, in his great love for others, would have marked out the child at a glance as the next piece of parochial work to be done, and done it.

The close of his ministry was a tragedy. Dr. Randall Davidson, who then had no sympathy with, or understanding of, Anglo-Catholicism, became Bishop of Winchester. Dolling had built magnificent St. Agatha's in place of the Mission church. The Bishop refused to dedicate it unless he would " bring his services into general harmony with the due order of the Church of England." It must be remembered that Dr. Davidson, as Dean of Windsor, had been saturated in Queen Victoria's distrust of Anglo-Catholicism ; to him she had deferred over many ecclesiastical appointments ; and between them they had effectually barred the road to high preferment to any but Low Churchmen.

He had assisted at the trial of saintly Bishop King of Lincoln for "ritualistic" practices. And he had been sent to conduct the services in Father Tooth's church when he was under "discipline," being turned away by the churchwardens. Dr. Davidson of those days was not the mellowed, sympathetic, helpful Primate whose memory we revere. Could he have foreseen the Malines Conversations which he encouraged as Primate he would have expired in horror. Dolling, who was ill, received the shepherd's crook on his head with a sound and resounding clump. The Bishop would not sanction a third altar. He condemned Requiem Masses. He required at least three communicants to be present at each celebration. He insisted on a new licence and, cruellest cut of all, charged Dolling with playing fast and loose with the Church's rules. There were protracted negotiations and efforts to mediate, but, perhaps hastily (for a sick man struggling with a tiresome and ignorant bishop would sooner fight wild beasts at Ephesus), the noble pastor threw himself to the wolves in January, 1896.

A dispensation ended, a shining light went out. Dolling was "unemployed." He was inhibited by two bishops. He wore himself out by writing and preaching to raise money for the Mission he could never serve again in person. That marks his sheer nobility of character. If we bow to the Dolling of Landport we must kneel to the Dolling exiled. He went to America, where his health was restored, but he declined to be Dean of Chicago. It seems a pity! He would have accepted the living of St. Mary the Virgin, Somers Town, but had not been the requisite span of time in the London Diocese. In the end they made him Vicar of St. Saviour's, Poplar, and there he died on May 15, 1902, at the age of 50. He was not a success at Poplar. He had burnt himself out at Landport.

A "Dolling Memorial Home" was set up at Worthing in his memory, and there his sisters went to live and labour. I, who have penned this memoir with an aching heart, served my first Mass in its sweet chapel of St. Raphael. I had come under the gracious influence of the Misses Dolling in a curious way. Their father had managed the estates of my mother's family in Ireland, and the Dollings and the Anketells (my mother was an Anketell) had played together in childhood. Many years afterwards, when my parents had fallen on hard times, and retired into the terrific privacy of Worthing, they lost touch. One day a lady called at our house for a servant's reference. She was shown into the dining-room, where the family portraits hung; and when my mother entered, the visitor cried: "Good gracious, who *are* you?" She was one of the Dolling sisters, and the old happy friendship was renewed, and I came into it. They gave me a new cassock when I went to college, and lamented that they could do no more, saying, "If only Bob were here!"

They were the sweetest women I ever met, and I know why they converted Landport. I need not tell the Catholic reader. I will not tell the pagan.

XIV

HENRY PARRY LIDDON

1829–1890

THE name of Liddon recalls the renascence of St. Paul's Cathedral (when it became a power it is not now) and the sunset of the age of golden preachers.

Captain Parry was Liddon's godfather, his father, Matthew Liddon, an officer of the Royal Navy, having served under Parry in the attempt to discover the North-West Passage.

Henry was the eldest son of a family of ten, born at North Shoreham in Hampshire on August 20, 1829. His childhood was uneventful. His favourite game was preaching in a surplice made of *The Times*. He was always quietly good, and his seriousness made his word count among his mates at the boarding-school in Lyme Regis, where he was sent when he was ten. He entered King's College School in 1844. A contemporary writes of him:

He always seemed to me an elder brother, who wished the young ones were more serious. . . . I always found him friendly, gentle, and considerate. So far as I can remember, he was at seventeen just what he was at twenty-seven, or thirty-seven, or forty-seven—sweet, grave, thoughtful, complete. Others, perhaps, may recall growth, change, completeness, gradually coming on him in look, form, mind, and character. I cannot. To me, when I heard him preaching in St. Paul's, or heard him speak at Oxford of more recent years, he was just the same earnest, zealous, affectionate, and entirely other-worldly nature that I remember at seventeen. The lines in his face may have deepened: the look may have become more anxious of late years. But, as a schoolboy, I always thought he looked just what he did as a priest. There was the same expression of sweet, somewhat fatherly, somewhat melancholy interest. He would re-prove, exhort, advise boys just as a young priest does in his own congregation. We expected it of him: and it never seemed to us to be in any way stepping out of his own business when he gave one of us a lecture or a sharp rebuke. We seemed to feel that this was what he was there for. He was entirely a priest amongst boys.

He won a studentship at Christ Church, Oxford, at the age of seventeen, fell under Pusey's influence and became an Anglo-Catholic. When he left Oxford he worked with Mackonochie under the rigorous Butler at Wantage; broke down; and then became first Vice-Principal of Cuddesdon, a college for ordinands founded by Bishop Wilberforce.

His work there was of short duration, for differences arose between him and the Bishop, and the opposition of Protestants and the nervousness of moderate Churchmen combined to make him relinquish his task. But Cuddesdon bore the stamp of his remarkable personality long after he had left. He set before the theological students an ideal which was unusual in days when it was possible for a man to be ordained with little or no training, on the strength of moderate success in examinations or merely family status. And ordinations left much to be desired, as one can see from the following letter written by a young priest in 1841, thirteen years before Cuddesdon was opened :

I was ordained priest by his holiness of Winchester on July 11th, at Farnham Palace. There were about thirty men ordained. The palace is a fine old place ; many of the men were lodged there during the examination, and all dined there every day. The dinners were sumptuous : all served upon silver. Oh, if some of the old bishops could have looked in !

I arrived at Farnham on the Saturday ; after dinner we were ushered into the private Chapel—a queer place, comfortably carpeted and cushioned.

The Bishop gave an *exposition* ; and then his chaplain offered up an extemporary prayer—such a prayer ! The Prayer-book was altogether discarded. The Ordination was conducted in the most comfortable manner. Great praise is due to the head valet for the orderly arrangements ; he was most indefatigable in his exertions to secure the ladies and gentlemen good seats ; and indeed I may say the same of the livery servants ; they were all motion—sliding about the Chapel in pumps—noiseless as cats. Nor should I forget the Bishop's Chaplain, who was especially polite to the elect few who honoured the ceremony with their presence.

Arrayed in full canonicals, the flowing sleeves of his surplice floating on the breeze which his flight from the drawing-room to the Chapel occasioned, he smilingly handed a galaxy of beauty and fashion to their cushioned seats. When all men were seated in breathless expectation the sleeves were heard in the distance, and presently appeared the Chaplain, leading in the Bishopess, the first of a long procession of children and maidservants ; all the candidates, except myself and one or two others, arose, and testified their respect. Lastly the Bishop entered (all men on the tip-toe of expectation) wearing the Order of the Garter. He smiled blandly—the menservants rushed to the Altar Gates—they flew open, the Bishop entered—they closed—the men-servants retired. A hymn was given out—the Bishopess arose and led the singing, leaning gracefully over the pew door. Even at the very moment when silence is kept awhile, the Bishop's wife commenced singing the *Veni Creator Spiritus*.

Released from the ties of Cuddesdon, Liddon began to develop his remarkable talent of preaching. Mrs. Butler had said, on hearing his first sermon at Wantage : " That young man preaches better than Archdeacon Manning." He bestowed immense labour on his sermons, and was spent and ill when he left the pulpit. Dr. Pusey became anxious. Liddon had been invited to preach in St. Paul's. He wrote to him : " You preach sermons an hour long at St. Paul's, and nobody hears you, and you are knocked up a fortnight afterwards. You have done nothing." Yet he could keep the boys at Harrow spellbound. An eyewitness writes :

His appearance instantly attracts attention. " He looks like a monk," one boy whispers to his neighbour . . . the Oxford M.A. gown, worn over a cassock, is the Benedictine habit modified by time and place ; the spare, trim figure suggests asceticism ; the beautifully chiselled,

sharply pointed features, the close-shaved face, the tawny
skin, the jet-black hair, remind us vaguely of something
by Velasquez or Murillo. . . . The vibrant voice strikes
like an electric shock. The exquisite, almost over-refined,
articulation seems the very note of culture. The restrained
passion . . . warns even the most heedless that something quite unlike the ordinary stuff of school sermons
is coming. The text is announced, " Remember now
thy Creator in the days of thy youth. . . ." We are
listening, for the first time in our lives, to a man inspired. . . .

For an hour . . .

Liddon played a prominent part in every controversy after he had been made a Canon of St.
Paul's through Mr. Gladstone (in 1870). The
cathedral then may be summed up in the words of
Charles Kingsley, twenty years earlier:

The afternoon service was proceeding. The organ
droned sadly in its iron cage to a few musical amateurs.
Some nursery-maids and foreign sailors stared about
within the spiked felons'-dock which shut off the body
of the cathedral, and tried in vain to hear what was going
on inside the choir. The scanty service rattled in the
vast building, like a dried kernel too small for its shell.
The place breathed imbecility, and unreality, and sleepy
life-in-death, while the whole nineteenth century went
roaring on its way outside. . . . Coleridge's dictum,
that a cathedral is a petrified religion, may be taken in
more meanings than one. When will life return to this
cathedral system?

It returned through the influence of Canon Liddon
and Dean Church. Dean Church was a noble and

gracious priest who had come to London " with
fears and with repugnance " at Mr. Gladstone's
urging. A biographer says :

Henceforward until his death he was one of the chief
influences in ecclesiastical affairs. He detested controversy and shunned public meetings, for he was a shy and
sensitive scholar, but his passion for righteousness and
truth burnt like a flame, and was felt on all sides. He
became, as it were, a " standard conscience by which men
tested their motives and their aims."

He and Liddon were twin-souls, and the wilderness of St. Paul's began to blossom like the rose.

In 1871 the Judicial Committee declared the Eastward Position at the altar illegal, and the Bishop of
London, Dr. Jackson, tried to enforce its decision
on St. Paul's. Canons Gregory and Liddon
announced that they would not alter their liturgical
practice, and invited the Bishop to prosecute them.
The Bishop climbed down. A year later Liddon
was involved in a battle royal with the Archbishop
of Canterbury, Dr. Tait. The Athanasian Creed
was attacked, and the attack was fostered by the
Archbishop. He fought the Archbishop step by
step, and on December 23, 1871, wrote to him :

If this most precious creed is either mutilated by the
excision of the (so-termed) Damnatory Clauses, or degraded, by an alteration of the rubric which precedes it,
from its present position in the Book of Common Prayer,
I shall feel bound in conscience to resign my preferments,
and to retire from the ministry of the Church of England.

Dr. Pusey announced the same intention. The controversy dragged on for a long time, but Liddon won the day.

He touched life at so many points that a rapid biography must do him scant justice, and to select episodes is a difficult task. Perhaps the most sorrowful period of his life was when the *Lux Mundi* crisis began to agitate the Church in 1889. He had been instrumental in the founding of Pusey House, Oxford, and had appointed Charles Gore as its head. It was to perpetuate Dr. Pusey's memory by being " a home of sacred learning, and a rallying point for Christian faith . . . at what, so far as we can judge (he said) must always be one of the chief centres of the mental life of the country." It was to " exhibit, as the old Colleges of Oxford were meant by their Christian founders to exhibit, solid learning allied to Christian faith and piety." Liddon " knew and loved (Gore's) general character ; knew that he was sound about the Incarnation and the Sacraments ; and did not suspect that he had constructed a private kennel for liberalizing ideas in Theology within the precincts of the Old Testament, and so much of the New Testament as bears upon it." The intransigent Liddon was horrified that the collection of liberalizing essays known as *Lux Mundi* should emanate from Pusey House. *Lux Mundi* was an " attempt to put the Catholic Faith into its right relation to modern intellectual and moral problems." It had an immense vogue. I do not think it helped anyone. When I was in a seminary fifteen years ago I read some of it. It is now as dead as mutton.

We must all wish to make the best, and not the worst, of a misfortune [wrote Liddon]. I do think it a serious misfortune, in itself, and for the sake of the Pusey House. Theology is not a matter of characters holy or attractive, or the reverse. It is a matter of propositions which are either true or false. And I cannot harmonize Gore's theory of our Lord's *ad hominem* arguments with any such belief in the perfection of His Human Soul as Catholic theology prescribes.

He capped this criticism by a magnificent sermon in St. Paul's. He wrote to Archdeacon Denison, a pugnacious but genial Anglo-Catholic who had been prosecuted by Protestants for heresy in proceedings that stretched from September, 1854, to February, 1858 (unsuccessfully to the Protestant cause), had left the English Church Union over the *Lux Mundi* dispute, and been throughout his long life (he lived to be 91) a very faithful upholder of Catholic life and practice, believing to the end in the catholicity of the Anglican Communion :

I have tried to tell Gore as explicitly as I can how wrong I think his language, and how gravely the *assumed* ignorance of our Blessed Lord's Human Soul on the subject of the Old Testament bears on the true doctrine of His Person . . . it is the high-road to Nestorianism.

While *Lux Mundi* distressed and even antagonized men like Liddon and Denison, Gore's later theological contributions have been unequalled in our age, comprehensible even to Fleet Street with its *penchant* for misunderstanding theology completely. None the less Gore suffered from the press, which always fastened on his "sensational" views (as in the case of the monumental *New Commentary*) and made him appear more revolutionary than he really was. He was a Catholic at heart.

The lucidity of his writing has helped the educated layman; and his unswerving stand against laxity of morals (particularly in the use of contraceptives) and in behalf of Church Order must ever command the gratitude of the Catholic Movement. Yet, at any-rate in his later years, he was more a critic of the Movement than an enthusiastic digger of wells choked up by our Protestant forbears. He saw it as something nearly fully developed, yet hardening in all sorts of wrong shapes; whereas, though the Movement is celebrating its centenary it is still in its infancy. He might have been a leader, but he never really receded from *Lux Mundi*. *Lux Mundi* sent Liddon to the grave in sorrow. On February 19, 1890, he wrote: "Dear Gore is deeply committed to a large number of young men who regard him as the clever inventor of a working compromise between Catholic truth and negative criticism, and who would be much grieved at his relapse into *consistent* orthodoxy."

Liddon died tragically, on September 9, 1890, worn out by writing an unfinished and massive Life of Pusey; reluctant to see friends; saddened by the death of Cardinal Newman (which affected him almost unnaturally) and despairing of, though faithful to, his Church. " He had lost all heart about the Church, and he was so miserable at the assaults on the Faith that he no longer cared to live."

No shelf of theology is complete without a set of his incomparable sermons, and although he was ever immersed in current affairs and controversies, and thereby in danger of preaching and writing the ephemeral, he has gained an assured place among masters of peerless English. I rank him next to Newman. He was a prophet, too.

If [he once said] the union of Church and State is to continue, it can only be when these changed circumstances are practically recognized—the Church asking for less in the way of support and privilege . . . and the State forgoing the claim to interfere with the Church's spiritual functions. Should Parliament, in the years which are before us, show an increasing disposition to treat the Church of Christ in this country as if she were merely " a department of the Civil Service," the consciences of faithful Churchmen will, however reluctantly, be driven to urge the separation of Church and State.

Again :

Our real danger lies in the direction of attempts to save the Church from Disestablishment and Disendowment by . . . destroying . . . what it has of fixed doctrine and discipline."

HENRY PARRY LIDDON

The views are the views of Dr. Hensley Henson, but the voice is Liddon's half a century ago.

Liddon was very human. He was always reading newspapers and violently disagreeing with them. If he had not become a priest he would assuredly have become a great Editor with fire in the heart of his prose. He loved children, but never married. He was a charming companion over a glass of wine, and had a delicious sense of humour. A friend once remarked upon a thick fog that had settled over London. Said Liddon : " Dr. Westcott must have come to town and left his window at Westminster open."

XV

FATHER IGNATIUS

1837–1908

ON November 23, 1837, four years after the Oxford Movement had begun, there was born at Trinity Square, London, to Francis Lyne, a merchant whose father had been Welsh and whose mother was Italian, by his wife Louisa Genevieve (*née* Leycester), a second child who was destined to blaze a trail across the pages of Anglican history ; be detested and persecuted by fellow-Churchmen ; win countless souls for Christ ; and raise up a memorial in stone which must ever remain a permanent reproach to the Church he served so nobly, and to the generations which have forgotten even his name.

Joseph Leycester Lyne was rather a precocious child, who early became oppressed by a fear of hell-fire, which was to haunt him for thirty years and then vanish by a revelation of the saving power of Christ. He seems to have impressed his masters mightily. One of them, writing his memory of Joseph in St. Paul's School, twenty-four years afterwards, said :

My recollections of Joseph Leycester Lyne are among the freshest and most pleasing reminiscences of well-nigh the third of a century's superintendence of St. Paul's School. You may say to all who ask (if any should ask a question)—Had he the usual failings of a boy ? that, in my judgment, he was most unlike all boys that I ever knew, with none of their pardonable short-comings, and more true holiness and spirituality of mind and character than usually falls to the lot of Christians, still growing in the grace of God in after years throughout this world's proficiency.

As a young man Joseph came into repeated conflict with his father, who disliked his High Church tendencies, but despite many ups and downs (emptying a Presbyterian church while, as a layman, in charge of a mission in Scotland, and driving all his own flock to the Presbyterians !) he managed to become a deacon. As he was much criticized in after years over his ecclesiastical status it is important to mention that, having scruples over his baptism as an infant, he was conditionally baptized at this time by the vicar of St. Peter's, Plymouth, taking a vow of perpetual celibacy.

Helped by friends he became an unpaid assistant to Canon Prynne, of St. Peter's, Plymouth, where he worked fruitfully. Dr. Pusey and Mother Priscilla Sellon (who re-established the religious life for women in the Anglican Communion) sympathized with his tendencies to monasticism. They became as convinced as he of his vocation to re-establish religious life for men, although it is evident that in time Dr. Pusey was frightened of his erratic ways. It is my purpose in this essay to stress the fact that what was erratic was accidental and superficial, and that a grave injustice has been done to Father Ignatius, as he was soon to style himself, by the overlooking, deliberate or otherwise, of the fact that he never turned back from any plough that he set his hand to.

Miss Sellon made him his first habit, which was intercepted and destroyed by his father ; and she made him a second. As yet he was a friar rather than a monk, assisting Father Lowder at the mission of St. George's-in-the-East. He became acquainted personally with all the inhabitants of the infamous Ratcliff Highway, where he was as fearless as he was tactless, going into disreputable dancing halls to announce, in a loud voice, that " We must all appear before the judgement-seat of Christ." Even more courageously, he threw away his chance of ordination to the priesthood by refusing to abandon the unusual habit that he wore on all occasions.

So I became a Benedictine [he wrote]. Two other people were willing to join me now. I was twenty-four years of age. My father was very angry, and refused to give me any further help. . . . I realized that I should be penniless. I had already drawn a very crowded congregation to Father Lowder's Mission Church, but I had made up my mind to break away from every tie. Relatives, except my mother, would have nothing to say to me. My bright prospects in the Church would be for ever ruined ; the world would say I was mad ; the Church would regard me as most dangerous, a kind of ecclesiastical Ishmael. . . . Yet I firmly believe God was calling me, and I must obey. . . .

Obey he did. To attempt, in what must be a short sketch, to follow his footsteps in detail is a task I cannot do. But, for the forming of a better opinion of this heroic deacon, I will outline him sharply in some of his astonishing crises (every day was a crisis, of some sort).

He was molested with violence by Protestant fanatics in the first house he founded, and was stoned in the streets. He shows no sign of wavering. He moved to another house, where he stayed, with his companions, for two and a half years. They were half-starved.

This morning [he writes] just as our firing was nearly all spent, a gentleman sent us two chaldrons of coke. One of the Brothers fainted away in choir on Wednesday last, and some ladies who were present in chapel sent, about an hour afterwards, a hamper of fish and seven-and-sixpence ; and so we had a good dinner that day.

At times his priory was surrounded by angry mobs. Police and armed supporters would camp around it. One day he set out for Rome, in search of health, with a quaint retinue, regardless of spiteful tongues— Brother Philip, Sister Ambrosia (to nurse him) and a little child of four years whom he had adopted as an oblate to the order. He was hospitably received by the Pope. Donald Attwater, in a recent book, is most amusing in this connexion. He writes :

Two men wearing the dress of monks, going about with an indeterminate female and a child in sandals and a white habit, would cause a sensation anywhere. In Rome it was a *furore*. Monsignori took snuff and looked down their noses ; ladies of the noble families put their heads together ; the superstitious shot out the index and little finger of the right hand. And the authorities sent somebody round to the Via Condotti to investigate. . . . Dr. Brownlow, of the Venerable English College, and afterwards Bishop of Clifton, was appointed to wait upon the distinguished visitor, and a religious woman was told off to take an adjoining room and chaperon Sister Ambrosia—Rome forgets nothing.

But when Ignatius returned to England he found his community at Norwich dispersed and his priory put up for sale. The Archbishop of Canterbury advised him to try to recover the property by action, but, though he struggled for twelve years, and spent all his inheritance (£12,000), he finally failed. Some accounts refer to a flaw in the title deeds, but the "official" biography by the Baroness Bertouch calls it fraud.

In August, 1866, Dr. Pusey invited the broken-down and lonely monk to stay with him in the Isle of Wight. Here his sorrow was turned into joy, as he walked along the seashore, while the melancholy roar of the sea whispered of the follies of the children of time. He was oppressed by the thought of Hell, his shattered health, his ruined life, when there flashed upon him, like a ray of evening sunshine, sinking softly on wild and wold, ere the tender stars come out to gleam in token of the infinite beauty of God, the thought that he was mistaken in trying to save his soul, for

Jesus Christ had done all that for him. He says : " I cannot tell the joy, the new life, the strength that came to me. ' My beloved is mine and I am his,' I could say with all my heart . . ."

Can we doubt this personal revelation when we consider the circumstances which surrounded the bewildered, shattered young champion of Jesus ? Note his unchangeability. To the end of his harassed life he walked in that radiance. If he was given to moods, and tempestuous actions, they must be attributed to the life he had to live, calculated to shatter the strongest of men, while he was one of the weakest. They were superficial. There never left his heart the joy that he gained on that memorable moment when he found his master on the shore in the evening.

The scene now changes. We find the undaunted monk essaying a task which only the faith which can remove mountains would embark upon. It is to build a monastery on a Welsh mountain, miles away from anywhere. The transport cannot get within four miles, and huge stones have to be dragged up in waggons. The workmen, inadequately supervised, quarrel and down tools. By fits and starts the work progresses, and the shell of Llanthony Abbey begins to appear. Meanwhile the monks are enduring hardships justly comparable to those of the Cistercians at Citeaux and Fountains.

Ignatius writes :

(We) went through incredible hardships at our first foundation here, I myself living in a cold wet shed, the only shelter for the Blessed Sacrament and myself for some time existing here ; the other monks living in a window-less draughty barn. . . . From 22nd July, 1870, until December of the same year, our first portion of the Abbey, the west cloister, remained unfinished. The kitchen fire, for cooking purposes, burned on the mud floor of the barn up in a corner, the smoke finding its way out as best it could. . . . As the winter frosts began our suffer-ings were great indeed. I myself often rose at 5 a.m. from my bed in the cold damp shed, the blanket that covered me really steaming with the damp. I had to quickly make my bed and ring the bell to call the brothers from the barn to come and sing Prime with me in my shed "the Abbot's Lodge." Of an evening, after supper and Vespers, we would kindle a fire on the muddy ground of the unfinished and desolate cloister, fastening up a blanket for a shelter from the cutting wind. We had gathered the wood on the mountain for ourselves, being too poor just then to procure coal.

And the while, in well-warmed episcopal palaces well-fed bishops wrote inhibitions, bidding him refrain from preaching in their churches ; and deans and archdeacons and the whole hierarchy of higher clergy spoke of him acidly or with jocularity over their wine cups ; and the people of England, who flocked to hear him in the Halls in which he was driven to speak, came to mock at a madman and remain to pray ; and dry-as-dust dons composed voluminous treatises to oppose Modernism, of which they were to become in time the champions, leaving him to beard the atheist in his den, and bid him come to Jesus. His magnificent debates with Bradlaugh and others at least effected this, that they compelled people to see that Christianity is a life rather than a creed.

In the fullness of time his Abbey was built, and like all cities built on a hill attracted pilgrims. Here one must notice a defect in his character which was, perhaps, the underlying cause of his failure to found an enduring Community. He was gullible to a degree. He took everyone at his own valuation, and so was perpetually surrounded by impostors as well as the genuine. The Community was thus exposed to constant disintegration and re-formation. Ignatius was so transparently honest that he simply could not understand how anyone could be deceitful. Towards the end of his life he swung to the other extreme, and became suspicious of everyone. Small wonder!

Another of his faults was an imperious temper. He was kind and affable in repose, but when aroused hardly responsible for his actions. He would, too, vanish on preaching tours for months while his monks, and the nuns whom he had established hard by, were inadequately provided for, spiritually and materially. This was a serious weakness. He was forced to pursue two irreconcilable paths, which he never doubted were the Divine plan for him; that is to say, he tried to be Abbot of a monastery, an office that can only be held wisely by an efficient and quiet administrator, with capacity to judge character, and a Missioner, plucking brands from the burning in Hull, Newcastle, Birmingham, Cardiff, Brighton, Worthing, and the United States of America, etc. And the

Mission work was done, again, for daily bread. It all worked into the scheme of things, but it spelt and provoked disaster. If someone had come forward with a substantial gift to endow Llanthony Abbey, it might belong to the Anglican Church to-day, and be a centre of vitality such as Cowley or Mirfield, or even if he had been a shrewd judge of character, for then he might have been assisted by an able monk. But the work was marred by the bickerings of his followers, who were quick to see and resent the intrusion of knaves. The right men cleared out while the wrong ones stayed—for a time.

This aspect of his work is pitiable, but dare we blame him? Scorned in his lifetime, he is forgotten by modern Churchfolk, and has lately been dubbed, by a biographer whom I suspect to be a Roman Catholic,

" the *reductio ad absurdum* of the reaction from eighteenth-century classicism and of the opposition to the new self-satisfied materialism and scientific rationalism ; . . . not indeed the last end, but a term of the Gothic Revival, of the Oxford Movement, of Romanticism, of Evangelicalism, of neo-Mediævalism, of revivalism in a general sense taking on a new and particular sense."

He so stresses his Victorianism that Ignatius would seem to be a religious version of Mr. Barrett of Wimpole Street. I suggest a simpler definition. Father Ignatius—*saint*.

The degree of his sanctity can be appreciated best by those whose work lies in the foundation of some colossal undertaking. They can feel for the frail friar in his weariness ; his eager search for funds ; his longing to be quiet in his monastery while the placards blazed abroad the information that he would preach in this place and in that, and reporters waited on his doorstep ; and, when quiet, in the restless urge that came upon him to win enough bread for his children, to whom the Church offered a stone. He cannot be understood by the simple and the scholarly and the stay-at-homes. It is illuminating, for instance, to find that in some of the histories of the Oxford Movement he is scarcely mentioned.

But I think that he was rewarded by Heaven. There are strange stories told, by those who knew him intimately, of visions and healings. Here is one, told me by one of his monks, who became a bus-conductor. I have told it in full elsewhere, but a mention must needs be made in this connexion. I quote my own words first, then his :

There were some boys who received their education in the Abbey. They were playing in the fields one summer evening, but abandoned their game and ran to Father Ignatius, crying out that there was a light burning in a bush. He calmed them, and ordered a watch to be kept before the altar by the monks of the Abbey and the nuns in the Convent near by. . . . The next day one of the nuns sent word that Father Ignatius had left the monstrance on the altar. . . . Father Ignatius went to lock it up, but it was not visible. . . . On that evening the boys saw the light in the bush again. The monks were assembled in the porch, where they sang an *Ave*.

LEAD, KINDLY LIGHT

. . . It was a foul night. The wind howled in the vast solitude. The rain teemed down. A thick pall of cloud draped the hills and the heavens.

Then—I quote the witness's words :

A wonderful light appeared in the heavens. It seemed to open out, and in the centre there then appeared the Blessed Virgin Mary. Her hands were outstretched, and the light from her presence was so radiant that the monks could hardly look upon it. The walls of the massive monastery became like glass.

I would comment on this vision only with two reflections. (1) Ignatius hated a lie. Others might deceive him ; he had no self-deceit. (2) Presumably a vision from Heaven would be a reward for sanctity and heroism. Who among priests and prelates in his days had more than he ? The splendour of his courage pales his contemporaries' valour (and there were giants in those days) into insignificance.

In connexion with the vision I once received the following letter :

. . . A rather extraordinary personal experience of mine with regard to him and his death may interest you. Except to a few intimate friends I have never talked of it. In 1889, owing to my adopting a profession Fr. Ignatius greatly disapproved of—I became an actor—for some few years our correspondence ceased. Several years later I happened to be in London, and being in Baker Street one afternoon, I saw a poster announcing a series of services by Father Ignatius at the Portman Rooms, and there being one that afternoon, I felt I must hear him once again, and went in and sat right at the back. At the end, as I was leaving, Mr. Charles Lamb, who for

years was one of his chief helpers in London, stopped
me and said, after exchanging greetings, the Rev. Father
spotted you and wants you to wait and see him. I did
so, and we had a long talk and renewed our friendship,
and I found that his views with regard to my calling had
become somewhat less austere. From that time we
restarted an occasional correspondence.

A few years later, I was living for a time in Bath, my
wife being an invalid. One Sunday evening we had had
some friends to see us, and when they were about to
leave, my wife suggested our walking with them thro'
the Park—it being a lovely evening. After saying good-
bye to our friends, as we were returning, I saw in the
twilight what appeared to be a statue of our Lady, with
a halo of light round it, in a group of trees, and the statue
seemed very familiar. I was, of course, convinced it was
some hallucination and said nothing, when my wife suddenly said, " What a curious place to put a statue of our
Lady. I've not seen that before—lets go over and look
at it." As her health was very frail and I dreaded the
effect of any shock, I persuaded her to put off seeing it
till another time. But the whole thing puzzled me, and
the next morning I rose early, went out and walked over
the same route, but as I felt sure, there was no statue.
When I got back my wife, who was not up, called me,
and when I went to her room, said, " You've been in the
Park." I said, " Yes." " There's no statue there ? "
I replied, " No." " Then look at that," and she handed
me the *Daily Sketch*, and the front page was headed " Death
of Fr. Ignatius," and the page was divided down the
centre, one side a photograph of the Rev. Father, the
other side a photograph of " Our Lady of Llanthony,"
the statue erected there in memorial of the vision. That
was the statue we both saw the night before in the Park
at Bath.

Two years later my wife died—alluding to that experience almost at the end.

Ignatius died, as he had lived, a monk, albeit a quaint one. He made a fatal mistake, as far as his work was concerned, in accepting ordination to the priesthood at the hands of a wandering old Catholic bishop, who was an adventurer. Thus he was finally discredited in the eyes of the Church that denied him the priesthood and ignored his appeals for the Sacraments for his flock. He died on October 16, 1908, murmuring, " Praised be Jesus for ever and ever," was given a wonderful funeral, and a number of critical obituary notices in the press. A fool like St. Francis, a hero like St. Benedict, a revivalist like Moody, a lover of souls like General Booth, an ascetic like St. Anthony the hermit, an orator as golden as Lacordaire, but withal a poor theologian, and as simple as a child, of whom his Church was unworthy. Alas ! She is awkward in her handling of saints and her saints cannot breathe in " Establishment."

XVI

ARTHUR HENRY STANTON

1839–1913

FATHER STANTON, one of the devoted parochial clergy who, during the latter half of the Victorian era, translated the Catholic Movement into a language that could be understood by costermongers, street arabs, sluts, and harlots, and the wayfaring, simple folk who, when converted, are the riches of the Church, was for fifty years an unpaid curate at the church of St. Alban the Martyr, Holborn ; proscribed, inhibited and persecuted ; offered a Prebendal stall in St. Paul's Cathedral in the evening of his days (which he declined with grace) and honoured at his passing by the most astonishing funeral within recent memory, his *cortège* being followed by all sorts and conditions of men, between immense crowds of weeping and awestruck people.

To write a short study of his life is to essay to describe in outline a mosaic of many colours. One must put oneself *into* it. From my youth up I have read the official biographies, whose pages are crammed with crises, humorous incidents (most of which have passed into the common store of religious gossip),

tragedies, persecutions, and scenes of sadness. I
know them all by heart, and that disadvantages me.
I am tempted to be formal, lest I spoil a wondrous
story by vain repetition; to begin at the beginning
with the Father as a child. Shortly before his death
he wrote to Father Russell, a fellow-curate:

Now I am in the house in which I was born, and old
experiences of sixty-eight years ago are renewed; for
then at 8.30 the drawing-room door opened, and nurse
appeared and said, "It is time for Master Arthur to go
to bed." Master Arthur got up and went sulkily to the
room opposite, the nursery, was put to bed and tucked
in. To-day nurse appears at 9.45, at the drawing-room
door, and says: "It is time for Father Stanton to go to
bed." Father Stanton gets up sleepily, follows nurse to
the room opposite, the nursery, gets to bed and is tucked
up. So history repeats itself."

Born into a well-known Gloucestershire family,
the Stantons of Thrupp, on June 21, 1839, he died
on March 28, 1913, seventy-four years young, as
some said, but, I fancy, a man of sorrows. He must
have been that. It is not given to one to be a famous
preacher, and a pastor of innumerable individual souls,
and a friend of youth, and to pass through bewilder-
ing changes over the span of fifty years, without
experiencing poignantly the discipline of sadness.
And this I assume from little incidents as well as
from the fact that he was subject to periods of gloom
as well as of light-heartedness. Towards the end
of his life he was seen, in a railway carriage, to cover
his face with his hands, as if in deep sorrow, and

the very way in which he could turn painful incidents, such as inhibitions by bishops, and the failures of those for whom he strove, into merry stories indicates a pathetic and beautiful tendency to hide his wounds in the mantle of self-forgetfulness. If he was spared the suffering that comes upon those who care deeply for the young, and are ever passing through the winter of disappointment which succeeds the spring-tide of hope, as the charm and promise of childhood wither in the stress of adolescence (for Father Stanton was not a "boys' priest") he must have known more intimately than most of us, as the march of life went on, the pain of Sir Bedivere, "companion-less, with the days darkening round him, and the years, among new men, strange faces, other minds."

He loved children, none the less, and they loved him; but he really *understood* youth, who evoked his deepest sympathy. Here is a story, which I have not found in any biography. It is said that, when due to preach at another church, he was late, and the crowded congregation passed through the dis-comfort of uncertainty. The hymn before the sermon was sung, and repeated, and sung again. Then he appeared, and hurriedly strode to the pulpit. "I am sorry to be so late," he said, "but it wasn't my fault. You see . . . I've been having winkles for tea. . . ." The tense congregation burst into merri-ment. "As I was going to the station," he went on, "I met a little boy, who said it was his birthday, and that I had promised to go to tea with him. I could not break my promise. . . ." And then he settled down to his discourse.

His tender heart must often have been torn by failure. *Punch* (I fancy) ridiculed him as " Stanton with hyacinthine locks, carrying a portable confession box," but the cheap gibers knew little of, and cared less for, his efforts to redeem the hooligans that used to swarm in the mean purlieus of old High Holborn.

Once [says a writer] a class of slum lads had been gathered ; one brought another, and so forth ; they came on Sunday afternoon for instruction, behaved quite nicely and attentively, and persevered . . . for a long time. Stanton at the commencement . . . began asking their names, but got no reply ; suspicious glances passed from one to another, and at last one answered, " We have all the same name, Jack—call us ' the Jacks.' " . . . They came one day bringing a large German lithograph of Christ blessing little children, framed ; they said that Stanton had been very kind to them and had tried to do them good ; would he accept this token of gratitude ? . . . After this presentation the Jacks simply disappeared, and no one saw or heard anything of them again. What did it all mean ? No one ever discovered.

Another time some of the slum lads said, " Father, next Friday is Good Friday, give us a treat." " No," replied Stanton ; " on Good Friday we come to church, we don't give treats, but if you come to church on Good Friday I'll think about the treat." They all came, and lustily sang " The Story of the Cross." " Oh ! I will follow Thee . . . unto the

goal," became, to them, " . . . unto the gaol."
" They kept their word," Father Stanton used to
say, " for they were every one of them in prison
before the year was out." He used to keep a cupboard full of clothes, and a pocket full of sixpences,
for the undeserving and the disreputable, among
whom he ranked himself, but he never gave reck-
lessly. He knew too much about human nature.

One other glimpse of his parochial labours. A
writer in the Protestant journal *Good Words* in 1868,
who had been courteously received by the vicar of
St. Alban's, Father Mackonochie, and put into the
care of Father Stanton for a tour of the parish, wrote :

I soon found that my animated interlocutor was no
mere dreamy . . . admirer of an ecclesiastical past gal-
vanized into seeming spasmodic vitality in the present,
but firmly convinced that his form of Christianity was
the only one that could get a real practical grip on living
men and women—especially on the degraded ones swarm-
ing around the clergy house . . . he seemed to find more
amusement than annoyance in the efforts made by emis-
saries of what he called " the Protestant party " to thwart
the tenants of the clergy-house in their parochial labours,
flocking after them . . . and placarding the parish with
posters, from whose small type stood out in bloated
capitals :

BEWARE !

CREEPING PRIESTS ! !

BLEEDING LIES ! !

He recounts a series of visits, friendly rather than

spiritual, two of which I quote as an example of that pastoral visitation obsolescent now in many parishes :

One more sample of parishioner's welcome will suffice. At the bottom of a narrow court we had knocked so long at the door of a little cottage, jammed up in a corner, without getting an answer that we were just turning away, under the impression that it must be empty, when the door was opened by an unshorn, lame old man. " Good-day, sir," he said, not looking over-pleased. " My wife's gone to the horspittle to git my physic ; but walk in, and set down." He hobbled before us into a little room, whose air smelt strong enough of tobacco to explain the secret of the old man's crustiness. We had, no doubt, disturbed the poor old fellow whilst he had been puffing away at his pipe like a locomotive, to finish it before he let us in. The conversation somehow turned on Ascension Day. The lame old man made a most lame attempt to appear interested in an assertion of its equal right with Christmas Day to be kept as a general holiday, and in the announcement that there would be four early communions at St. Alban's on that day, for the convenience of work-men who wished to communicate before proceeding to their work. The epochs of the Christian year had a very faint hold on the old man's mind, save as associated with personal material benefit. If he could have been told that Ascension Day would bring him roast beef and plum-pudding and a pot of beer, his appreciation of its claims to respect would have been marvellously stimulated. His stolidity changed into attentive listening with droll sud-denness when he was informed that henceforth he would be allowed a weekly dole out of the offertory.

I have kept the visit that struck me most for my last record. At the top of a squalid house lay two small-pox patients, in the same room with a corpse disfigured by the same dreadful disease. I started back with a sick shudder when I ascertained who and what were the occupants of that room ; but my companion entered it as calmly, to all appearance, as he had entered any other. Whilst he was in that awful chamber, with the dying and the dead, I stood at an open window on the landing below. At a workshop on the other side of a dirty little yard, in which the sunshine seemed to stagnate, carpenters were whistling music-hall tunes over their planes and up-curling shavings ; up the staircase every minute came the filthy, blasphemous language of a knot of sluttish women, squatting on the step of the open door, uttered with as little *malice prepense* as when the decently bred use " the " or " and."

Stanton's appeal, as I have said, was to the poor and outcast. He had no fine intellectual capacities. His early career, first at Rugby and then at Trinity College, Oxford, had been uneventful. Though of fine physique, and beautiful to look upon, he was no athlete, either. But he stood the test of war in the trenches of slumdom magnificently, from the day when he joined Father Mackonochie, in December, 1862, in the old thieves' kitchen that preceded St. Alban's as a place of worship, to the day when that lovely church had become a city set on a hill, an oasis in the Anglican desert. As in the first days " Yah " and " O Jerusalem " were shrieked down during service time, so in the later the Protestant persecutions made a ruder noise, with a persistency that must have often been insupportable. He stood by Mackonochie throughout the persecution, and he stood by St. Alban's, and the hosts of friends who found a home in its hallowed walls, and the postmen in his famous Guild of St. Martin, when Mackonochie was driven to resign. One of the noblest incidents in his great career was when, Father Suckling having come to be his vicar, he went on unmoved by a new subordination. One of the bravest was when, Mackonochie having been suspended, and he admonished to conform to the trumpery judgment that he should wear no vestments at the altar save (as he called it) a common choirboy's surplice, and use plain wheaten bread, he suspended the service of Holy Communion, and led his huge congregation across Holborn Viaduct and through Newgate Street to St. Vedast's Church, where a Solemn Mass was sung, at which he preached. And one of the funniest was when a visitor objected to the smell of incense. "Well," said Stanton, " there are only two stinks in the next world : incense and brimstone ; and you've got to choose between them."

When he died all London was moved, and those who had set him at nought and mocked him were silent, at last, and little children and ragged old women threw bunches of flowers in front of his coffin. The *Pall Mall Gazette* published the Memorial verses that follow.

> Cross the worn, patient hands upon his breast,
> The hands so swift to comfort and to bless.
> Let the tall tapers round about him glow ;

ARTHUR HENRY STANTON

The Knight of Christ has entered on his rest,
The sword laid down—the struggle and the stress
Give room to peace that none may trouble now.

Father, who kept the banner of Christ unfurled,
For fifty years of humble prayer and praise
Here in the London streets you loved and trod,
A challenge to the spirit of the world,
We shall go softly, softly all our days—
Knowing your prayers will help us up to God.

He was a great preacher [said a writer] as well as a
great parish priest, and he was a very great actor. He
had real dramatic genius, which was much helped by his
very striking appearance, and he had one of the most
beautiful—I use the word advisedly—smiles I ever saw.
. . . He was always at the call of the sorrowful. If
anyone was in trouble, there was always " Dad " to turn
to. Others might fail, but he at least was sure.

XVII

MARY SCHARLIEB
1845–1931

BORN in London, motherless from birth, this apostolic woman was brought up by devoted relatives, meeting, after leaving boarding-school, a law student of the Middle Temple, Mr. Scharlieb. They married and went to India.

Possessed of a deep sympathy and power of intuition, she was overcome with horror at the sufferings of Hindu and Mohammedan women. She felt a call to help them—a call not at all appreciated by the medical authorities, who did their best to oppose her. But she stood firm, and was finally permitted to work in the Lying-in Hospital in Madras. There, without assistance, and in the teeth of opposition, she began to study for her medical degree. It was the more difficult, too, because she was by this time the mother of three children. Yet, after three years of unceasing labour, in and out of hospital, she received from the Madras College her Licentiate of Medicine, Surgery and Midwifery. She then came to England to take the final M.B. and Bachelor of Surgery degrees; went to Vienna and then back to Madras. There she managed, again in the teeth of opposition, to found a hospital exclusively for caste Hindus and Gosha Mohammedan ladies, of which she took charge.

But she was over-working. Not only had she the hospital, but many duties as a general practitioner, and many lecturings. In 1887 her magnificent career in India came to an end, and she returned to London, with broken health, to win a fresh reputation for selfless devotion. She succeeded Mrs. Garrett Anderson at the New Hospital for Women. In 1902 she became gynæcologist to the Royal Free Hospital.

What is so astonishing is that, throughout her arduous life, she was far from robust. There was a radiance in her face, always, as if she had just come from prayer. There is many a woman in London who recalls her with gratitude, for in poor homes the remembrance of a gracious doctor never dies.

I remember vividly how prodigal she was of her valuable time when I needed her advice on one occasion, and how she sought in her shelves for books for me, and let me take them away as if unmindful of the risk of lending books to even the honestest folk! And I remember, too, how she stood at the door when my visit was over, and begged for prayers for a dying daughter.

Such women are the salt of the earth. They contrast in startling manner with others of, perhaps, equal brilliance and personality, who are uninformed by Catholic wisdom and unwarmed by prayer; spending many days in labour for which none rise up to call them blessed. Such are sometimes they who write autobiographies. In such a work I read the other day: ". . . in the light of reason and pure logic, a saint is a very tenth-rate human being, and St. Francis as lamentable a failure as the Emperor Nero."

Throughout her long life, consecrated to religious service, she won many battles. To her is due, very largely, the equal status of men and women in the medical profession. It is good to remember that women doctors have this freedom as a result of the Anglo-Catholic Movement, represented by her. She ceaselessly opposed birth prevention, writing helpful books for mothers, letters to the Press, and giving lectures. Oh! that she could have gathered together and corrected those amiable but undiscerning prelates who, at the last Lambeth Conference, dared to trifle with the Church's moral law, so that now even the clergy find upon their breakfast tables price lists of contraceptives to which their purveyors have attached an episcopal *nihil obstat*. Gentlest of women, I once heard her say that Dr. Stopes's books were "pink sugar," and made her "feel soiled" when she read them.

For many years she acted as Hon. Consulting Physician, Vice-President, and Member of the Medical Missions Committee of the S.P.G. A "beloved physician." If St. Peter stands at the golden gates for you and me, St. Luke must have been there for Mary Scharlieb, most splendid of the daughters of the Catholic Revival!

XVIII

FRANK WESTON
1871–1924

SHORTLY before the War the public was brought into familiarity with a word which will be recalled with ease on account of the difficulty of pronouncing it. I refer to " Kikuyu."

The Bishops of Mombasa and Uganda, without reference to the diocese of Zanzibar, had joined in conclave with the various Free Church denominations that were working in Africa, to find a solution of the problem of how best to meet the spiritual needs of Africans who moved from one territory into another. The dual menace of Islam and the white man who exploited blacks, together with the tug of tribal customs, seemed to them (and the average Englishman was quick to agree) to constitute a difficulty that made domestic ecclesiastical differences relatively absurd. They felt that at all costs a way must be found for the African trained by the Anglican Church in Uganda to have Communion in another territory where the Free Church was the sole representative of Christianity.

We are accustomed, in England, to adapt ourselves

to denominational difficulties. In Africa they are highly embarrassing. Essential Christianity appears sharply outlined there against a background of ignorance and false religion and sin. What appear at first sight to be accidentals of Christianity tend to be regarded as immaterial. That such a view is very natural we should be the first to admit if our parish, with its sundered Christian units—Church, Roman Catholic, Methodist, Salvation Army, Congregational, Baptist—were taken into the heart of Africa and left to preach the Gospel. In the teeth of opposition, and in the face of primitive passions, we should speedily become vexed over apparently artificial divisions.

Some sort of Concordat was come to and submitted to the (then) Archbishop of Canterbury. But the Bishop of Zanzibar, Frank Weston, who is the subject of this memoir, felt that unity could not be reached by a short cut; that the old garment could not be patched without a worse rending; that interior unity must precede exterior.

He was training his Africans to believe, for instance, in the Apostolic Succession. How, then, could he send them forth to receive the ministrations of those who disbelieved in his conception of the Church ? " He did not believe that ' a Church ' with an indefinite faith, with no determined rule of life and a haphazard form of government, would be strong enough to weld Africans together, to uplift them as a race, or to defend them against being exploited by Indians and Europeans."

He wrote, accordingly, to the Archbishop of Canterbury, denouncing the Bishops of Mombasa and Uganda for the part they had played in " Kikuyu," and charging them, formally, " with propagating heresy and committing schism." If he failed to do justice to the fact that their scheme was tentative, and not in operation, they, for their part, cannot be excused for having ignored the existence of the Diocese of Zanzibar. The upshot of it was that the Bishop of Zanzibar's position was upheld, but, as the War had broken out, Kikuyu meant little to any but anxious Churchmen. The Anglican Communion once again steered clear of the rocks, although her break-up had been prophesied, but Frank Weston, who dared to turn her from danger, was in disgrace.

Meanwhile, he was gravely disturbed by the growth of Modernism in the home Church. *Foundations* had been published, and the man-in-the-pew, convalescent from Kikuyu, was discussing Mr. Streeter's curious theory of the Resurrection. The Bishop of Hereford, Dr. Perceval, a famous Headmaster, had defended the Modernists, and collated Mr. Streeter to a stall in his cathedral.

Suddenly the whole of Christendom was startled by a document which Frank Weston pinned upon the door of his cathedral in Zanzibar (as Luther nailed his Theses to the door of Wittenburg Cathedral), announcing that he and his diocese were no longer in communion with John, Bishop of Hereford, and all who adhered to him. Here was a first-class crisis. Dr. Perceval defended himself in the columns of *The Times*, and gravely rebuked a junior bishop for being a junior. In a headmasterly manner he went out to rap the knuckles of an irresponsible schoolboy, not realizing that to point to the youth and inexperience of his opponent was merely to trail a red-herring across the track.

Then, to Frank Weston, came the crowning blow. Dr. Hensley Henson (who since his elevation to the episcopate has moved steadily towards Catholicism from the advanced trenches of Modernism, and is the most fervent of all advocates of disestablishment) was made a bishop, after a stormy protest by many Churchmen. Modernism had seemingly triumphed. Frank Weston replied by his *Christ and His Critics*, and began to think of retiring from his See to live a simple Christian life among his Africans.

Most people at home, having no idea of his beautiful character, or of the conditions in Africa which moved him to act spectacularly, assumed that he was a firebrand, in love with excommunications and anathemas. They called him the Zanzibarbarian. But he had the heart of a little child as well as the mind of a master theologian and the courage of a Christian warrior. Here is an example of his tenderness.

He was sometimes obliged to excommunicate Africans who led scandalous lives.

There was one very sad case of a man [writes Canon Maynard Smith, in his biography], the godson of a dead missionary, who had been one of the Bishop's boys at Kiumgani, and afterwards a teacher. The awful solemnity took place in church. The candles were dashed down and extinguished, but when the Bishop came to the terrible words : " We do hereby cut you off," he could not complete the sentence, but broke down sobbing. All the congregation sobbed with him, while the bell went on tolling for the doom.

There was the essential Frank Weston, never shirking an awful duty, whether in his relations with the episcopate at home or the simple African in his diocese. Vision is for the future, he would say, pain for the present.

His war force of Africans was a marvel. Experienced officers used to gape in amazement at the way in which he controlled an awkward squad of two thousand men. Whatever he was commissioned to do, that he did. He received the O.B.E. Yet it was only through the intervention of the Archbishop of Canterbury that he received his war medals. He was a constant fighter of injustice. His pamphlet, *The Black Slaves of Prussia*, will never be forgotten in Africa, and his later one, *The Serfs of Great Britain*, has not been forgiven ! He hated the colour ban. He used to say that Christ was a coloured man.

It was, however, at the Lambeth Conference in 1919 that he came into his own. At the first Anglo-Catholic Congress he had played an insignificant part, but the unforgettable scenes which took place in the

Albert Hall, when a vast number of men and women
pledged themselves to the service of Christ, and cast
jewels and riches into the alms-sacks, renewed his
confidence in the Church of England. He went
from the Albert Hall to dominate and sway the
counsels of the bishops assembled at Lambeth. He
entered the assembly a suspected and discredited
prelate. He chose a seat, and sat, and listened. He
rose at length to speak. One can picture the solemn
prelates of every clime and country leaning forward
to see and hear the tiresome *enfant terrible*, in anticipation of a storm of wordy criticism. They were
given the surprise of their lives. Here was no thin-
lipped, harsh, narrow-minded bigot, intent on grind-
ing a diocesan axe in and out of season, but a bronzed
and finely built man who spoke as never man spoke
before. There was something about him which
made them listen and learn. He addressed them
with learning, common sense, humour and a friendly
tenderness which took their breath away. He spoke
to them, some of them aged, and all of them steeped
in the spirit of autocracy (for monarchical infallibility is by no means the prerogative of the Pope !),
as a father might speak to his sons, but with such a
winning gentleness that they were impelled, in the
end, to see a vision and send out the famous appeal
for unity. He left them under a spell. Had he been
at the last Lambeth Conference the terrible mistake
of sanctioning birth-prevention in certain circumstances would never have been made to distress

Churchmen, demoralize the nation, and fill the coffers of purveyors of means of iniquity.

A few years passed by, and he was back again, worn out, but engrossed with the Anglo-Catholic Congress of 1923. Here he became the leader of the Movement at long last, such a leader as it has lacked since Newman went out in the forties. His musical voice could be heard all over the Albert Hall (there were no " mikes " in those days). Every gesture he made evoked a storm of cheering. For the first time, I venture to say, many of us who beheld him (and I sat at his feet in worship) came face to face with an Apostle. None but he could have sent the famous telegram to the Pope and survived it. Messages were being sent to Kings and Prelates . . . Christ had told us to love our enemies . . . why should we not revere the Supreme Pontiff ? So he thought, and in a moment a message was drafted and put to the crowded house, and sent. Whether it went by way of Westminster at once, accompanied by a Cardinal's comment, or was delayed until it was pointless, I know not. I have heard whisperings, which it would be good to have stilled. But here was the message :

Sixteen thousand Anglo-Catholics in congress assembled offer respectful greetings to the Holy Father, humbly praying that the day of peace may quickly break.

The next day he was torn to pieces not only by the press, and the Protestant underworld, but also by

Dr. Frere and many friends, but he never regretted his action. "I am very tired," he said, as he went back to Africa. He died not long afterwards, on November 2, 1924, at the age of fifty-three. If I say next to nothing in this memoir of his early days (he was born on September 13, 1871); his evangelical upbringing; his boyhood at Dulwich College; his years at Trinity College, Oxford; and of the making of the missionary at St. Matthew's, Westminster, it is because my space, not my admiration, is limited, and his greatness was revealed in the latter days. There has been none like him for Apostolic unction in the history of the Catholic Movement, and since his passing none has led as he.

But many a humble priest has been enheartened, and many a layman awakened by the man and his message, and his last charge to Anglo-Catholics, which follows, should both effectually make ritualistic squabbles seem futile, and give the lie to ignorant critics who suppose that Anglo-Catholics care only for chasubles and candles.

. . . I say to you, and I say it with all the earnestness that I have, if you are prepared to fight for the right of adoring Jesus in His Blessed Sacrament, then, when you come out from before your tabernacles, you must walk with Christ, mystically present in you, through the streets of this country, and find the same Christ in the peoples of your cities and villages. You cannot claim to worship Jesus in the tabernacle if you do not pity Jesus in the slum. . . . It is folly, it is madness, to suppose that you can worship Jesus in the Sacrament and Jesus on the throne of glory, when you are sweating Him in the bodies and souls of His children. . . . You have your Mass, you have your altars, you have begun to get your tabernacles. Now go out into the highways and hedges, and look for Jesus in the ragged and the naked, in the oppressed and the sweated, in those who have lost hope, and in those who are struggling to make good. Look for Jesus in them, and, when you have found Him, gird yourself with His towel of fellowship and wash His feet in the person of his brethren.

His official biographer, Canon Maynard Smith, records the effect of the charge thus:

His splendid voice rang out through the great hall. There was a note of yearning in its tones, you could not escape from his insistent passion, his passionate love of God, his consuming pity for the sons of men. A great wave of emotion flooded the assembly . . . respectable dignitaries, afraid of compromising themselves, were swept away by the common enthusiasm. It was not only what he said, it was his character and its reality which dominated the crowd. . . . Professor C. H. Turner, looking back upon that evening, said, after Frank's death . . . "I think the Bishop of Zanzibar was the greatest man I ever met: I know that he was the greatest orator I ever heard."

XIX

ARTHUR TOOTH
1839–1931

ON March 5, 1931, a sunny old saint passed peace-fully away, and the curtain fell on an epoch. Up and down the press there were obituary notices, for Arthur Tooth was " news " because he had been in prison. They missed the point entirely. Arthur Tooth was " news " because he lived in perpetual sunshine, and because he bridged a gulf.

The gulf that he bridged divides the great Trac-tarians from the modern Anglo-Catholics. This is not the moment to describe the Movement, but it is relevant to say that many of the younger Anglo-Catholics are anxious over their leaderless condition. Upon them has fallen the mantle of such illustrious fore-runners, who have written history over the face of the world-wide Anglican Communion. There were giants in those days, and there are few, if any, now, perhaps because the general stature is higher.

Arthur Tooth was one of the giants, and he towered into the present day. He was born at Swifts Park, Cranbrook, in Kent, on June 17, 1839, and was educated at Tonbridge School, and Trinity College,

Cambridge. He was fond of sports and travel, and once was lost in the Australian Bush, finding his way back by the stars. After several short ministries he accepted the derelict living of St. James's, Hatcham. He repaired and furnished the church and began to draw a congregation. He founded a Community of Sisters and an orphanage, which served as the choir school of the church. His teaching was simple, lucid and definite, and he introduced, within a few years, most of the customs and usages which are normal in moderate churches to-day, but were then considered to be of the essence of Popery. He founded, also, the Guild of All Souls, which lives to this day.

The quiet growth of his parish in devotion was, however, rudely checked by Disraeli's ridiculous Public Worship Regulation Act, 1874, designed to put down " the Mass in masquerade." It was enthusiastically supported by Queen Victoria, Lord Shaftesbury, and Dr. Tait, Archbishop of Canterbury. A new court was created to try cases, and was presided over by an ex-Divorce Court Judge, Lord Penzance. Prosecutions were begun, with the result that a number of clergy were imprisoned. The average length of imprisonment was 147 days. Before his own, Father Tooth read the following charge to his people, in consequence of which the Rev. Randall Davidson,* the Archbishop's chaplain, who was sent to take services, was refused admission to the choir by the churchwardens :

* He became Archbishop himself.

LEAD, KINDLY LIGHT

In the Name of the Father, and of the Son, and of the Holy Ghost. Amen. I, Arthur Tooth, Priest of the Church of England, Vicar of this Parish, desire, in the present distress, to make profession, in the face of God and of my people, of my willing obedience to all lawful authority, as binding every Christian by the Word of God and the law of his Church.

It has become my duty, in consequence of certain proceedings taken against me in a Secular Court, in respect of the manner of worship of the Church of England, to enter at this time my Solemn Protest against the exercise of Secular Authority in matters Spiritual.

And further, in full reliance upon the Christian intelligence of my people, and upon their loving readiness to suffer for the truth's sake, I hereby call upon them to recognize no Ministrations in public Congregation, nor any discharge among them of the Office and Duty of Cure of Souls either in the immediate present or in the future, other than my own, or of those acting in my behalf under my authority.

I make this call upon my people as the lawfully and canonically instituted Priest of the Parish, not inhibited therein, nor deprived thereof by any lawful and canonical authority. And I implore them, and if need be, require and charge them to bear steadfastly in mind that all ministrations and discharge other than my own are schismatical, and are an invasion and a robbery of the rights of the Church of England. Witness my hand this third day of December, being Advent Sunday, in the Year of Our Lord, 1876.

ARTHUR TOOTH, M.A.

On the next Sunday there were 700 people present at High Mass, the clergy and congregations of St. Alban's, Holborn, and St. Peter's, London Docks, having gone to St. James's, Hatcham, to support it by a visible token of sympathy. In the New Year the riots broke out, arranged by the Protestant underworld. And here, both as regards the imprisonment that was soon to rob St. James's of its Confessor's presence and the frightful scenes that took place Sunday by Sunday, when windows were smashed, worshippers assaulted and the Mass was disturbed by blasphemous yelling, I prefer to record Father Tooth's own words, fifty years after.

He told me the story one day, after I had walked through a swirling mist to his orphanage for boys at Otford, Kent. The mist made me think of the mist of the years which separated the old man from descendants, like myself, of his contemporaries. We are so different from them. They were austere, self-disciplined men of prayer, who studied, and visited, and built up famous parishes with divine patience. We, their children, have a lilt in our lives. They wept, but we laugh. They lamented over a Church that seemed to be dead bones, but we are a mighty army. They abstained, but we, perhaps more in the spirit of St. Francis, who called for a dish of almonds and whipped cream on his death-bed, enjoy modern luxuries—smoking, for instance. " Will you smoke ? " said Father Tooth to me, in his richly furnished study, hung with tapestries and pictures and relics collected from all over the world. " Have one of mine." I had one of his. It was dry with age. I should not have been surprised to know that he had bought the packet as a dissipation when he came out of Horsemonger Lane Gaol.

While the ancient weed blazed up he told me the story. " I had a fine, united congregation at St. James's, Hatcham," he said. " Sunday by Sunday I had to say Mass with booing and hooting for response. Hooligans were sent down by the Church Association to disturb us, and, if possible, break up the service. They were paid half a crown each, while boys got a shilling. They would keep their hats on throughout the service, and often there were fights between loyal members of the congregation and the toughs. Then a charge was brought against me, and I wouldn't appear. They could find me nowhere, and thought I had slipped through their fingers."

His eyes twinkled and his mouth twitched.

" I went to Maidstone," he continued, " to await arrest, but nothing happened, so I came back to London, and there they took me. Horsemonger Lane Gaol doesn't exist now, and what do you think they've done with its bricks ? " I could not think. " Built a church with them. But the gaol was a shocking place for draughts." The old man shivered in remembrance, and then merrily laughed. " I didn't mind, and I always was obedient. I expected to be there for years, and I must say they treated me fairly well. The warders didn't know what to make of me. I felt uncomfortable only when I exercised in the yard. There I was seen by the women, who used to wonder what the gay old dog in a clerical collar had been up to. They let me keep my clothes."

Through the windows I could see that the low-lying mist had cleared, and out in the sunny field there sounded the click of bat on ball, and the shouts of merry youngsters.

" I have trained fourteen hundred boys," he said, a little sadly. " They're all over the world. Some are doctors, some are clergy, some are lawyers. Some have been very bad boys. . . ." He said that as if he loved them more dearly than the good ones. " Sometimes they write to me. Sometimes they come to me."

" What happened when you came out of prison ? " I queried.

" One day," he replied, " they told me to go, and, being always obedient, I went. I got back to Hat-cham and found my church bolted and barred. I broke in by a window, and said Mass in the usual way, as it's now said in thousands of churches, with altar lights and vestments. But it could not go on for long, and the congregation was broken up. My opponents bought the advowson, and put their own man in."

He retired with shattered health to a house at Woodside, Croydon, where he began a noble work for orphans, and among inebriates and drug addicts. In 1924 he moved to Otford where he continued his work for boys in a fine estate of some eighty acres, and there he died. If so sunny a saint could be said to have a shadow over his life it was cast, during his later years, by the unsuccess of his efforts to give away his magnificent mansion and grounds, first to the Anglo-Catholic Congress, and then to the Diocese of Southwark, to the S.P.G. and to the Archbishop of Canterbury, as a training centre or rest house for clergy, and to see erected in Canterbury Cathedral a worthy memorial to Thomas à Becket, his favourite saint. He had offered £10,000, and a committee was prepared to find a like sum, but negotiations were protracted, and the Chapter rejected the design by Mr. Comper. Father Tooth died, and the chance was lost for ever.

He left £33,000 to the two Sisters who had helped him to conduct the orphanage, which is being carried on.

It was my privilege to become the friend of this old saint, in later years, and to take my choirboys year by year to his orphanage, where he would feed them with pies full of sixpences, and then send them out to play cricket. Every few moments during dinner, which we took on the lawn, he would come strolling out from the kitchen with a hot pie under his arm. He loved little children, and they loved him. There was an intangible bond between them —the link of childhood, natural and supernatural. The year before he died my little slum choristers had been naughty, and I was obliged, with many apologies, to cancel their outing. It was the first year of the Choir School romance, written of in my *Ten Years in a London Slum*, and *We do see Life*. Small faults were large ones, therefore; and one did not feel that boys in a tiresome frame of mind should have a lovely treat. I have regretted, ever since, that we did not go. He was waiting for us. He wrote on a postcard two words—*Piteous Pies*. The head choirboy, very sorrowfully (for the discipline worked wonders), wrote an apology.

After his death, at the age of 91, a beautiful cricket bat was sent me by the Sisters. He had meant to give it to my boys, and it had stood in his study until he died. When the Choir School was dedicated last summer by the Bishop of London it was presented to the chorister who had made the most progress in " musick, manners and vertu."

He had no place in the bosom of his Mother Church in his lifetime, but first place in the hearts of children. And one day, when the Anglican Communion has learnt to recognize sainthood, we shall find in her Kalendar the following feast :

" Arthur Tooth, Priest and Confessor."

When they laid his body to rest, at St. James's, Elmers End, there was snow on the ground—a pall of purity.

XX

THOMAS ALEXANDER LACEY
1853–1931

I INCLUDE him amongst my heroes, not because he was a great scholar who could, with the blessed faculty of a born journalist, open his store of learning to the wayfaring man (though a fool)—he used to write as " Viator " in the *Church Times*, which, after many years, to the regret of its readers and the loss of the Church, closed its columns to him—not because he was an unrivalled expert in mediæval Latin and Canon Law—not because he did a wonderful work among girls in Penitentiaries ; certainly not because he was a born controversialist, with remarkable powers in debate ; but because he did outstanding work in the cause of Reunion, and that in despite of ugly rumours that the ignorant wove around him. It was a piece of work which forms an important chapter in the history of the Anglican Communion. Amongst all Lacey's activities the visit to Rome and all that preceded and followed it was what made his reputation.

He was born in Nottingham on December 20, 1853. In his childhood he owed much to a remarkable mother who, at the age of twenty-one, was left penniless with two young children, Mary and Thomas, both under the age of three. She could have had help from his grandfather, but that would have imposed upon her the painful discipline of sending her son into an unsatisfactory environment.

Taking her courage in both hands she began a School. Her noble and charming character exercised a great influence upon the girls who came under her care.

Thomas and his sister were necessarily left much alone. They were clever children, and soon made the most of the few books that came their way in early childhood. They devoured the Bible, *The Pilgrim's Progress* and Goldsmith's *History of England*. In her spare moments Mrs. Lacey laid the foundation of her son's remarkable familiarity with the Latin tongue, little guessing that he was one day to sway Pope Leo XIII by it. He was soon given a free place in the Grammar School in Stoney Street, Nottingham, where he became at length the head boy, working for a scholarship at Cambridge. His Latin papers in the Oxford Senior Local Examination brought him an offer, however, of an exhibition at Balliol, which was to influence his whole life. He went up a shy, raw, conceited boy of seventeen, making friends at once with another " fresher " named Charles Gore. Many times in his writings and by other means he spoke of Gore's influence upon him, and of his devotion to his tutor, J. H.

Green.   Amongst his contemporaries were Asquith, Milner and A. L. Smith, afterwards Master of Balliol. He left Oxford to work at Wakefield Grammar School, and was ordained deacon to St. Michael's in 1876 by the Bishop of Ripon, continuing his scholastic work.

Early in life he had become a Catholic, in spite of the overwhelmingly Protestant surroundings of his childhood.   He was led into Catholicism in this way. At a history lesson his headmaster, a priest named Cusins, whom he loved and revered to the end of his life, asked the class for a definition of Transubstantiation.   One boy of very Protestant upbringing said : " The idea that the bread and wine in Communion is changed into the body and blood of Christ." The master replied : " No, that the *substance* of the bread and wine is changed into the *substance* of the body and blood of Christ."   His master's definition seemed so clear to the bright young scholar, and indeed the only possible explanation, that he accepted it without hesitation, and never thereafter questioned it, and all the other elements of the Catholic Faith, as he came in contact with them, fitted in of themselves.   At Oxford he had secretly endured many hardships, in his anxiety to burden his mother as little as possible.   At Wakefield he had to suffer for his convictions.   The Bishop of Ripon refused to ordain him to the priesthood unless he would promise never to wear vestments.   He refused, and it was over two years before he was priested.   In the end a compromise was made, he resigned his curacy at St. Michael's, and the Bishop consented to ordain him priest so that he could take work in another diocese. It was an absurd compromise, but he was glad to help the Bishop out of an awkward position. Father Benson of Cowley was shocked at it. A few days after his ordination he said his first Mass at Horbury.

Then he went to St. Benedict's, Ardwick, in the Manchester diocese. Typhus was prevalent, and he came into contact with it day by day. There were no compulsory powers of removal, and he used to go into houses to persuade the stricken inmates to allow him to carry them into ambulances. His personal influence was often the deciding factor.

He successively became assistant master of Denstone College and was made a Fellow of the College of St. Mary and St. John, Lichfield; vicar of St. Edmund, Northampton, and vicar of Madingley, Cambridge. In 1903 he resigned the last-named benefice, as his journalistic and other activities, consequent upon his famous work in Rome (a description of which I reserve for my " curtain ") was taking up so much time that he felt he could not do his duty to his parishioners adequately. In addition, his family (for he had now three daughters and two sons) was growing too large for the vicarage. He went to live at Highgate, becoming chaplain of the House of Mercy there. On the death of the Rev. Edgar Smith he became Warden and began a remarkable work among fallen women which endures to this day as a memorial of his saintly life. He remained at this task until made Canon of Worcester in 1918.

Whilst he was living in Highgate he did a great deal of open-air speaking on Parliament Hill and in Finsbury Park, with great success, being always ready with answers to hecklers. In 1905 he worked for many days (and nights !) in the production of the *English Hymnal*, translating ancient Office Hymns into magnificent English, and writing some original ones, of which the best known is " O Faith of England," three verses of which he wrote on the top of a bus to the patter of the horses' hoofs. Are they not audible throughout these lines ?

> O Faith of England, taught of old
>   By faithful shepherds of the fold,
> The hallowing of our nation ;
> Thou wast through many a wealthy year,
> Through many a darkened day of fear,
>   The rock of our salvation.
> Arise, arise, good Christian men,
> Your glorious standard raise again,
>   The Cross of Christ who calls you ;
> Who bids you live and bids you die
> For his great cause, and stands on high
>   To witness what befalls you.

He overworked himself so seriously that he broke down, and through the kindness of friends, of whom Lord Halifax was one, he was invited by the Brockle-banks to go as their guest for the round voyage to Calcutta on one of their fine new cargo ships. He said good-bye to his family, expecting to be put over the ship's side before she should reach Calcutta, but at the close of the cruise his health was restored, and he began to send to the *Church Times* his " Bishop's Letters," which many consider his cleverest and most brilliant productions.

After he became Canon of Worcester (in 1918) he had no opportunity for several years to use his vast experience in Rescue Work. He was never even put on to the Diocesan Council for Rescue and Preventive Work, but that ignoring of his great talents was only in keeping with the way in which the Church wasted him. He ought, by virtue of his vast ecclesiastical knowledge and general learning, to have been raised to the episcopate. Had he been a " careerist " he would no doubt have tempered his brilliant wit, his rapier-like debating powers, the satirical skill which could make matchwood of the most apparently learned and carefully presented case. But he was *himself*, always, and perhaps better served his generation by remaining a free-lance. The Church does not know how to use free-lances. It was surprising that he was made so much as a Canon. It brought him real happiness, therefore, to be invited to become chaplain of the Diocesan Rescue Home known as Field House, which is worked by the Sisters of the Holy Name, Malvern. In spite of advancing years and infirmity he would rise at 6.30 on three mornings of the week to say Mass there. He loved his work, and everybody at Field House loved him. One very rough girl once said that somehow Dr.

Lacey always made them understand things. The women sweeping their door-fronts all along the road came to know and love him, as he strode along morning after morning, unconsciously saying his prayers aloud all the way, and stopping on his return to stroke all the cats that used to come out to greet him. (He had a great love for cats, and there was one in Field House that seemed to know at once when he arrived to say Mass, and was with difficulty excluded from chapel.) Then he would turn into the cathedral to hear the Mass there.

He always enjoyed a joke against himself. For example, he never could be taught to sing in tune, but was most assiduous in singing the Preface and other parts of the Mass. At the annual cathedral choir supper he used to entertain the lay clerks and old choristers with stories about his singing. One that never failed was that of a priest who said to him : " I do love to hear you sing the Mass, Lacey, it wafts me across the seas to those delectable lands where they have never heard of the detestable Anglican tradition of singing in tune."

He had the clearest views on all the acutely controversial subjects, and often at clerical meetings, when all were at cross-purposes, would restore order by a deft analysis of what each had been trying to say. Here, for example, is a letter about gambling which is far too shrewd to be lost. As usual, it is undated, perhaps because he lived mentally in so many different ages :

The conclusive answer to your argument is this, that to bet for the sake of getting money is not gambling at all. It comes under a different category. It is excluded by the Bishop of Southwell's admirable definition which I find the more satisfactory as I look closer into it. Everyone sees the absurdity of calling a book-maker, or the proprietor of Monte Carlo, a *gambler*. They do it as a business—to get money. Again, if a regular gambler is attacked on the ground of the costliness of his amusement, his favourite—and truthful—answer is that if the play be fair and the chances even losses and gains are bound to balance on the average. Hence it is absurd to look for gain in gambling. Again, I find on investigation that in gambling circles a man who is suspected of playing for (?) . . . stakes is fought almost as shy of as a man who is suspected of cheating. They don't like to play with him. All these facts and many others are inconsistent with any definition but that of the Bishop of Southwell, i.e. that gambling is betting *for the sake of the excitement*. I have occasion in the earlier part of my paper to show that if a man bets for the sake of living without working he is incontestably sinning. I show this not on socialistic principles, which I have quite ceased to believe in, but purely on theological grounds, and if, as is usually the case, he is counting on " luck," he adds the sin of profanity. I afterwards show that no such betting ought to be called " gambling." No doubt illogical men will go on condemning " gambling " without stopping to think what the word means, and meaning themselves something quite different, but there is no reason why logical people should follow their example.

It was in the year 1894 that T. A. Lacey began to stride into European fame by his composition in perfect Latin of a dissertation on English ordinations.

To do his task well he had bravely wrenched himself mentally from his Anglican setting, and thought with the mind of Rome. The document was composed with a view to its being read by the Pope and His College of Cardinals. He says, " To throw oneself into a hostile position, to argue upon the assumptions there treated as indisputable, and to wrest from them an affirmative conclusion, was a new employment from which one might naturally shrink. But the work seemed to be needed." Things moved apace in the next year, as some eminent French ecclesiastics took up the Anglican case. The Pope determined to investigate the whole question, and Lacey, with Father Puller, was " briefed," as it were, by Duchesne and Portal to elucidate the Anglican contention. They conducted affairs with extraordinary wisdom, holding no official position as touching their own Church, but supported by the confidence and approval of the Archbishop of York, Mr. Gladstone, and Lord Halifax. They laboured in vain, for, as all the world knows, Anglican Orders were declared invalid, a decision which disappointed him deeply, but had been skilfully guarded against by his and Father Puller's independent attitude. Never once had either of them appeared in the rôle of supplicants.

He often said that he never worked so hard in his life, and the occasional reference in his diary to " a nightingale singing all night " shows how toil restricted his hours of sleep. After several months, he wrote home saying that his brain was reduced to pulp.

He suffered much from home sickness, longing to be back with his wife and bairns; but it was a period full of interest and novel experience. He had the privilege of being present, on one occasion, at the Pope's private Mass, which he said daily. His Holiness's custom was to hear Mass said by a chaplain immediately his own was finished. Leo XIII said his Mass with a tremulous piety that deeply awed Lacey. The chaplain who followed said his in the worst Italian style, and the Abbé Portal, who was with Lacey, was shocked and said: " *Si je disais la Messe comme ça devant* mon *Superieur !* " Lacey never forgot that Mass of Leo XIII, and no doubt his own very devout way of celebrating was partly influenced by it.

It is a curious fact, indeed, that he should have been called to play such a momentous part in the history of Christendom, while in his own Communion he was never made more than a Canon. But now that he has gone many recognize that a prophet has fallen in Israel.

A few weeks before he died he sent me a letter of assent to a suggestion that he should contribute a volume on " The Meaning of Pain " in a series I was to edit. He said that it was a subject upon which he thought he could write helpfully. Alas! suffering itself wrote " finis " to a plan which might have enriched the Church with another of his master-pieces. But that he would have wished, for, although he was a great author, a great journalist, a great fighter, he was above all else a great priest. *Ecce sacerdos magnus, qui in diebus suis placuit Deo, et inventus est justus.*

He died on December 6, 1931, conscious to the last, fortified by the Blessed Sacrament, commending his soul to God.

XXI

MOTHER KATE

THE foregoing pages have done scant justice to
women of the Catholic Movement, save to Christina
Rossetti and Dr. Scharlieb, and (by allusion) to the
Misses Dolling and Charlotte Yonge. This is a
serious weakness. Yet, while the devotion of
women has been a strong foundation, their level of
sanctity being higher than that reached by men
(perhaps because they do not fear to commit themselves when convinced, or mind that criticism at
which men quail who would courageously go into
warfare), their work has been unspectacular. It has
been along four lines—the quiet round of parochial
labour ; nursing (the effect of which needs no description) ; literary (but to no large degree, for the Catholic
Movement can boast few giants among women) ; and
conventual. The heroines of whom one would fain
write have been withdrawn from the public gaze.

Yet my book would be sadly incomplete if it gave
the public the notion that Heroes rather than Heroines
have been the order of the day, for the true facts
are otherwise ; and I therefore turn with pleasure to
magnificent Mother Kate, being the more happy to

write about her because she came into touch with some splendid Heroes to whom I meant to devote chapters until I awoke, with a shock, to the knowledge that my space was filled. Her tale is told in *Memories of a Sister of St. Saviour's Priory*, a book long out of print.

Katherine Anne Egerton Warburton was born on March 24, 1840, in the heart of Cheshire, in a village on the banks of the Mersey where, as she says, the cottages were smothered in damson-trees and "outlying farms stretched away over a wild Moss, redolent with sweet gale."

There were many odd, old customs [that she witnessed with wide-open eyes], such as the Rush-bearing, when there was a sort of Wake, and carts decorated with flowers went about, and people were more or less tipsy. This took place about the middle of August, and [she supposes] was a relic of the festivities of the Feast of the Assumption. On November 1st the wilder young men used to go about with lanterns at night, one wearing a horse's skull, which they called "Old Nobs," and went to the farmers' homes for drink or money.

She recollects them coming into the kitchen and prancing about, much to the delight of the maids. "That must have been the relic of the Soulers, being the eve of All Souls' Day."

Her father was a keen Tractarian and wore a surplice.

No one would believe [she says] the storms elicited by preaching in a surplice! "Sacrament Sundays" were few and far between. Etiquette in many parishes prescribed that the squire, the parson, and other dignitaries, with their families, should communicate first, and then the common throng.

She remembers that there was once an uproar because a farmer's wife went to " First Table."

But the Tractarian leaven was working . . . a most wonderful episode was the story of the heroic deeds of the little band of Priests at St. Saviour's, Leeds, during the cholera visitation of 1849–1850. . . . Sisterhoods were just making their first trial and (she remembers) hearing a good deal about Miss Sellon and her work at Devonport.

It was not until 1867 that she began to take a deep interest in these things, as a result of a mission conducted by young Mr. Henry Collins among the roughest and most sinful people in the London Docks. But Mr. Collins seceded to Rome. Years after, when she was a Sister at Haggerston, he visited her and begged her to leave the City of Confusion for the City of Peace, as Papists are accustomed to refer respectively to Canterbury and Rome.

She describes a Churchman whose name is now forgotten, Mr. Rowland Egerton Warburton, of Arley, Cheshire—a kinsman. He was called " The Squire."

And a veritable ideal squire he was, seeming, as Lord Halifax once said of him, to be a perfect combination of a good churchman, a good landlord, a keen sportsman, and a man of literary tastes. In the thirties and early forties, when Keble, Pusey, and Newman tried to pull the Church out of the depths into which she had sunk, when laymen, as a rule, took very little part in Church matters, the young squire of Arley flung himself with the keenest interest into the Tractarian Movement. When he rebuilt the Hall, he attached a beautiful chapel to it. And in days when daily prayer was scarcely heard of, the household assembled within its walls, and a surpliced choir chanted choral Matins. Never was the squire missing from his place, and on hunting mornings he always appeared in scarlet and buckskins. Right on in his old age, so long as he was able to get about, in spite of the blindness which came upon him during the last twenty years of his life, it was touching to see him kneeling still as he had done for past years, and when at last he was no longer able to get about, he was carried downstairs and wheeled in a chair into chapel. He was one of the first members of the English Church Union . . . he was a keen sportsman, a daring rider—" little Rowley the steeplechase rider," as he is described in a local song of some sixty years ago. . . .

He wrote a volume of *Hunting Songs*. It is refreshing to find that all clergy who hunted were not spiritually slothful; this man cared for both the souls and bodies of his tenants. The allusion to Lord Halifax comes almost as a shock. One is so used to knowing that the " Lay Pope " of the Church of England is over ninety years of age that one fails to realize how many Heroes he has met and what a history of the Movement he could write.

It was at Arley that Katherine met the Rev. Charles Gutch, afterwards vicar of St. Cyprian's, Marylebone, who suggested that she should try her vocation at St. Margaret's, East Grinstead. So to

St. Margaret's in the heart of the country she went, although she longed to be in the throbbing heart of a city. And thus we come to Dr. Neale, the immortal priest-journalist and confessor.

I had meant to give Dr. Neale a chapter, and to that end had studied his voluminous letters. Alas ! I am thwarted by space, but well so, for what could I say better than she has said of him whose lovely translations of old hymns whisper down the corridors of time, whose prolific pen, in tale and treatise, was more powerful than a two-edged sword to convince and convert (it is inimitable still), whose trust in Providence led him to take wild jumps and land on his feet; the intrepid restorer of Sackville College, whose slogan was : " What is possible may be done, and what is impossible must be " ?

Young, ardent, enthusiastic, large-hearted, full of sympathy, a poet, a scholar, a student, and, to crown all, gifted with intense energy of purpose, never, to our judgment, did man seem more utterly out of place than was this young Priest, in the midst of (his) surroundings . . . he seemed utterly wasted and thrown away in (his) bucolic *entourage* (but) was to kindle a light which, by God's grace, has shone far and wide. . . .

He had become Warden of Sackville College.

Below the town lies a green belt of pasture-land, beyond which the great brown ridges of Ashdown Forest sweep the southern horizon . . . away eastward, a richly wooded green country stretches away till it melts into the blue distances of Reigate and Dorking. Beautiful as this lovely view is to look at, scattered over the vast area, buried in the woods and out-of-the-way wilds, were innumerable hamlets and isolated cottages, badly built, badly drained, far from human help and resource, when fever or any illness attacked the inmates. Day after day, as he paced, as his custom was, up and down this terrace, and looked out over the fair scene, his heart burned within him at the thought of all the miseries of these wretched cottages. . . . Scholar, student, poetically imaginative man though he was, he was not one to simply sigh and sympathize, and then let things take their course. He no sooner felt an existent evil than he tried to find a remedy for it. And so it came to pass that God put into his heart to try to form a Sisterhood whose special object should be to go out into these poor cottages, to live with, and nurse the sufferers under their own roof. It seemed a wild idea, a hopelessly impracticable one. People were stiffer, and more set in their own special grooves than now-a-days, and society was more aghast at any departure from routine. Besides, the Bishop had inhibited him for having a Bible with a cross on the cover, and a cross and candlesticks on the Communion Table.

I should like, had I space, to speak in his own words of the foundation, but must hurry on, resting content with a picture of Dr. Neale by the hand of Mother Kate. It is inimitable.

What [she says] I remember so specially about Dr. Neale is the sort of energetic way in which he threw himself into all the active work of the Community. . . . If it was a fine, bright half-holiday, and he thought it would do (his) orphans good to take them for a ramble into some distant wood, or to see a quaint church in some outlying village, he organized a party, and escorted two Sisters and the older girls to view whatever might be the object of interest, and while pointing out all the beauties of a wooded glade, where the crisp young bronzy oaks stood knee-deep in blue-bells, or some eminence which had been a Roman camp, or some soft gray distance from which rose the tower of some church, he intermingled with these, anecdotes of his travels in Dalmatia, Spain, and a hundred and one interesting places, full of stories of the Saints . . . The winter of 1860–1861 was a bitterly cold one, and there was much distress among the poor cottagers. He organized the Soup Kitchen . . . if a Sister was nursing in some lonely, out-of-the-way hamlet, he would always find time to go and see her, at least once during the period of her nursing. . . . Though so very particular about the neatness of the orphans' dress, he never seemed to notice what he wore himself. His usual costume was a cassock, and white bands such as John Wesley's portraits have, and out of doors he invariably wore a college cap. But he was perfectly unconscious of drops of wax from the candle being on his cassock, or of frayed and worn edges, and equally unconscious of it when a new one was provided for him. His own study was a marvellous place, literally lined with books—great folios, unsightly duodecimos, parchment bound, leather bound, every size, every variety, every age, every language—treating chiefly of Ecclesiastical History, Ecclesiology and Hagiography, thronged the shelves from floor to ceiling. And these were not enough ; cross shelves filled up the middle of the room, packed and crowded with books, so that there was barely space to squeeze round from the door to the little fireplace in the corner, over which hung strange and valuable ikons, brought from Russia and Greece.

Such was the man whom they stoned, because he was an Anglo-Catholic !

After the solitude Soho, sickening, sinful, sottish

Soho, where she was sent to assist at St. Mary's in Charing Cross Road, which they are seeking to demolish now. Her memories of her early days there are very touching, especially so to me when she writes of the kind of children I met so often in the Somers Town of long ago. . . .

Dear visions of the past! How their faces rise up from the cloudy memories of bygone years, and one wonders where they now are, and what they are doing! . . . How well I remember Farden's first appearance in our school—a tallish, red-faced, black-haired Irish boy, out of the very Irish court opposite. His real name was Johnnie Grady, but he was introduced to me by his *nom de guerre* of *Farden-a-dozen*, " 'Cos, Sister, his mother, she sells apples on a stall on the Dials, and Farden, he gets all the rotten ones and sells them a farden (farthing) a dozen to the kids!" Farden never had very much to say for himself in our presence, but I believe he was the hero who led the others on to war in every raid on sweet stuff, and old women's apple stalls, and in every street fight. He disappeared entirely from the scenes after a year of our acquaintance, most likely being provided with a residence at Government expense. Certainly his lean prehensile fingers looked as if they must close on every article that came within his reach. He was one of the costermonger race. Watkin came from a family who got their living by the hod and shovel. Square built, rough and determined, he was the massive supporter of the lithe and wily Farden in all their forays. He, too, after a little while, was lost sight of in the ever-shifting, surging crowd of humanity which ebbed and flowed in Soho and S. Giles.

Billy Day, a fair-haired, apple-cheeked lad, was a sort of aristocrat, as his father owned a coal shed and a cart and pony, and Billy asserted his dignity in all the glories of a coal-smudged face, with the same conscious pride as an Indian brave puts on his war-paint. Mr. Billy was altogether rather too grand a man for us to have much to do with, still he condescended from time to time to give a grimy look into the schoolroom, and to join, in a sort of *dégagé* way, in any lark which seemed particularly interesting—never forgetting he was the son and heir of W. Day, coal dealer.

Fatty! well, I know nothing more of him than that he was Fatty, the bosom friend and sworn companion of Farden. I never knew what his name was, or where he came from. He resembled a calf's head in his face—fat, white and small-eyed: his clothes were more burst out than those of others, because they had the daily friction, not only of joints, but of solid fat. . . .

And Lygo, my poor, dear Lygo! Oh, what a big cowardly lout you were! Your comrades called you Bullocky, on account of your enormous head, thatched with shock manes of hair, and your large, grave, round eyes, resembling those of an ox. And yet you, the prince of louts, had the sweetest, prettiest little fairy of a sister that ever danced at the Olympic Theatre! You, I believe, got on during pantomime season as some sort of an animal, I never exactly ascertained what. Do we not remember you lumbering into the schoolroom one afternoon, with your knuckles to your eyes, sobbing and roaring, " Farden's hit me! " and little Punch from Newport Market, who reached nearly to your elbow, running up and saying, " Never mind, Bullocky, I'll lick him for you after school." I believe Punch made some excuse for both his friend's cowardice and his big head by saying, " Bullocky had tried to smoke some cigars one day, and all the smoke got into his head and had never come out again."

An organ-blower being wanted for the church, Lygo was promoted to that office, for which he was to receive two shillings a month. Should pressing and important business prevent his being at his post—such as helping his father occasionally, who was a scene-shifter at the Olympic Theatre, or, I fear, sometimes business on his own account in the rearguard of the forces of Messrs. Farden & Co., on a foraging expedition in Newport Market—he was to pay another boy a penny a night to take his place. A sharp little fellow, called Brads, from the Prince's Row Mission, was usually his substitute, but after several wrangles over the pence which Brads claimed and Lygo was unwilling to hand over, they came to a regular dispute, which the boys decided was to be settled by single combat, after dark, in the lonely purlieus of Soho Square. Brads, yearning for revenge and pennies, could not control his impatience till the settled night, but pursued Lygo after church, and, amidst an admiring circle of choirboys, attacked Lygo (who was twice his size) in the street. Lygo, roaring and howling, fled, pursued by the wasp-like Brads, and never rested till he was safe in his mother's room up three pair of stairs. His organ-blowing days were, however, brought to a premature end by his bringing a pocket full of hot jam tarts to church one Sunday night, intending them for refreshment during the sermon, and upon the organist expostulating and confiscating these dainties, he flung himself on the floor and kicked everyone who came near him.

. . . Once a week one of the clergy came in to catechize the children, and on this occasion an evil spirit seemed to have taken possession of Lygo. He fled underneath a gallery at the far end of the room, singing at the top of his voice the then popular song, " Oh, Bob Ridley, oh ! " in answer to all the questions, and neither force nor argument could dislodge him for a long time. At last we sent Farden and Watkin into his lair, one at each end of the gallery, and they, both seizing an arm, pulled him contrary ways, while he kicked and roared and yelled, and the glass roof above was crowded by court and other boys, pitching down stones and shouting, "Oh my! look at old Bullocky going to get a clout. I say, Bullocky, here's your father a-coming." The news spread round and one elder brother—the expertest thief in the neighbourhood—came to the school door, swearing he should come out without a caning, while the other, a soldier, on furlough, rang at the door of the Church House, saying he "hoped they'd wallop his brother well"; it would do him no end of good. And he got the "walloping" before he left.

At Easter there was a terrible visitation of small-pox in Soho and S. Giles. A number of the children were laid up, and the school had to be closed in consequence. Some of our workers in the home also caught it, and had to be nursed until they could be moved into the country. I had gone away for a few days' rest and change, returning one evening late in April. Doubly dingy did dear Soho look after the blue skies and pink and white apple and pear blossoms, and banks of primroses under the budding hedgerows that divided the newly ploughed fields, where the rooks stalked in solemn procession along the freshly turned furrows, from the woody coverts where the rabbits scudded over the tender young grass. There in the country everything was bright and sunshiny, and spoke of renewed life and spring; but, as I turned out of the bustle of Oxford Street, down the narrow, dusky windings of Crown Street, all seemed black and hushed, to speak of death rather than life, of decay sooner than of spring.

The dear old classroom had been whitewashed, and the haunted old house cleaned and renovated, and, after a discussion of plans for work, etc., we retired for the night. Ring, ring, came the bell—sharp, repeated rings, as of somebody who wanted something, and not one of the runaway tinkles given by some of the louts who shacked about the public-house opposite. And we found it was a poor woman, in very great and terrible distress. She lived in Rose Street: her husband and children had, and were still having, the small-pox, and a child of three was lying dead. By some negligence on her part, the body had not been removed, as it should have been, to S. Anne's Mortuary, and now the husband declared he would cut his throat unless it were taken away, as the child had been dead five days.

"There is nothing for it but for us to go," said Sister Mary. "You"—to the woman—"go home, and we will both be round directly." Provided with a roll of wax taper and a box of lucifers, we turned out into the street; a still, dark night, for the Easter moon was in its last quarter, and the white stars scintillated in the deep blue sky in cold contrast to the yellow, flaring gas lamps down below. The entrance to the court opposite, usually blocked up by a crowd of ragged, villainous-looking young thieves, was empty; they were all outside the theatres, picking pockets. The public-house across the street was within a quarter of an hour of closing, and the din of voices rose and swelled most audibly, mingled with here and there a piercing shriek or laugh from some poor wretched girl. Outside, on the kerb, a faded-looking woman, thin, haggard, wrapped in a ragged shawl, was singing plaintive songs in a rich contralto voice, for which she might get a few pence, and now and then, when the publican was in a good temper, he sent her out a little something by the potman.

When we turned into Rose Street, all was quiet, and inside the open doorway of No. — everything was pitch dark. We lit our coil of wax and stumbled up the shallow, old-fashioned stairs to the top-floor, from whence proceeded a sickening odour of chloride of lime. Inside the room everything was splashed with and steeped in it. A bit of candle burned feebly in a tin candlestick, showing a tub, half filled with a heap of clothes in chloride of lime ; a bed, a mere heap of rags, in one corner of the floor, containing two children, thick out with small-pox ; in the other corner a bedstead, on which lay the little dead child. Crouching over the fire, wrapped in a shawl, was a gaunt-looking man, his face also seamed and scarred with small-pox, and his bleared eyes glancing every now and then with a half-fierce, half-frightened look at the form on the bed. The wife was moving up and down, wringing her hands and crying wildly.

We asked if the Parish authorities would not fetch the body away, and the man gruffly replied, " So they would if *she* "—meaning his wife—" would have seen about it before ; now it is too late, they would not come," and if he had to spend the night with that body in the room, he'd make an end of himself as sure as he was a living man ; and then followed abuse of the woman, mixed with half-frightened execrations about spending one more night with a corpse. Sister Mary promptly sent the woman out to see if anyone could be got to fetch a coffin, " and we will go round to the mortuary."

After ten minutes waiting, with the children wailing on the floor, the man shuddering and insisting that he would destroy himself unless the body went out, we heard the wife's steps returning, followed by the heavy, lumbering tread of a man, and she re-entered the room, together with a rough, brick-laying sort of individual, reeling and lurching in, with a pipe in his mouth and his hat all aslant on his head. After much drunken protestation, he was induced to accompany us in quest of the coffin.

It must have been considerably past midnight when we knocked at the door of the mortuary in Dean Street— knocked and knocked and knocked almost hopelessly— till at last the door opened and an old crone put out her head. On the object of our errand being explained, she said she had been expecting the coffin to be fetched, and had waited up until 11.30, and no one had come, and now she had a bad cold, and had put her feet in hot water, and what did we mean by knocking her up at this time of night, etc., and very much more to the same purpose. However, at last she consented to give the man a shell in which to fetch the poor child.

When we got back the woman declared she could not touch the child to lift it in; the man, whom the night air seemed to have made drunker than ever, could not be tempted to do so, and she said to her husband, " Them two sweet creatures will put the little dear in," so we wrapped the little body in the sheet, put it in, and tied down the lid with a piece of old list. We could not trust the man to carry it downstairs, but managed it ourselves, and along as far as Greek Street, he tumbling and rolling along beside us, muttering and murmuring to himself. At the corner of Greek Street we put the coffin down to rest a minute, when a man came up and asked whether it was a dead body we were carrying, as it was an illegal proceeding. On our telling him all the circumstances, he roughly ordered the man to put the coffin on his shoulders instead of " letting those two females do it," and so we got it with difficulty along, by dint of walking close beside, and putting our hands on the coffin to steady it.

It was a weird night's work, walking slowly through the dark, silent streets, with our companion stumbling along, every now and then threatening to put his burden down and fly; the man who had stopped us joined in the little procession; we found he was an undertaker living close by, and, we suppose, was therefore naturally attracted by the sight of a coffin, and we were very glad of his presence, as we felt it compelled the man to go on, and not throw up the affair, as he seemed disposed to do. We were indeed truly thankful when we arrived at the mortuary, and after much and repeated knocking again aroused the old woman, and placed the poor little burden in her charge. Our friend, the undertaker, called round the following morning, and made sundry inquiries, and, I believe, had reason to be satisfied that we could not have acted otherwise than we did.

The years sped by, and Katherine found herself at Haggerston, and Father Mackonochie's constant visitation began to cheer the common round and trivial task. Mackonochie was the intrepid first vicar of St. Alban's, Holborn (under whom Stanton served), whose life was fretted by persistent persecution, arranged by the Church Association. No matter how involved he was in lawsuits, he would find time to enter into the details of the Sisters' work at Haggerston. After awhile they were but a remnant, as their chaplain, Father Tuke, " Poped," and caused them " Holy-See-sickness." In spite of Mackonochie's care of the bereaved Priory the majority of the Sisters went over, while Katherine was working in Plymouth. They owned the conventual buildings. She says :

. . . sad and sick of heart, I journeyed up to London. Arrived in Ash Grove, and preparing to ring the bell of St. Mary's Priory, I was beckoned by Sister Louisa, who appeared at a door opposite, and I found that through Father Mackonochie's exertions a small house had been secured as a refuge for the Sisters, the Priory itself being the property of the seceders. . . . Left by our comrades in arms, deserted by her, who, as our leader, not only here, but in the past years in Soho, judge how we felt !

> They left us for ever,
> Calmly advising us, follow my way ;
> As it were nothing those true links to sever,
> As it were simply but wishing " good day."

Yes, they had left us, well therefore uniting
    Band we together more firmly in one,
Fighting the battle they ought to be fighting,
    Doing the work that they ought to have done.

Yes, they had left us, but God had not left us ;
    God had not left us, and God will not leave :
No ! not a jot of our hope is bereft us,
    Fight we more earnestly, now that we grieve——

. . . Some of us felt it to be almost impossible to continue work in Haggerston in the very teeth of the Roman
Secession. . . . Better leave the field entirely, and return
to the Mother Home at East Grinstead, or concentrate
ourselves . . . at Plymouth. But Father Mackonochie,
firm of will and purpose, determined the work *should*
continue. . . .

Continue it did, but they had to move. To remain
opposite the deserters was too painful and confusing.
Another house was found and a new chapter begun,
in abject poverty, as the seceders had all the money.
Katharine, now " Mother Kate," says : " . . . we
struggled on through our first year, and young, and
full of hope, we rather enjoyed the struggle. . . .
Oh, the pleasure of finding a farthing in an old
coat when we had not a penny in the house. . . ."

The Sisters slept in one room, their beds touching
each other, their only dressing room the shelter of
a cupboard door ; whilst she slept on a table. At
times their only food was cabbage, gained by selling
old bottles at the rag and bone shop.

Here I must leave the dauntless Mother, whose
devotion during the small-pox epidemics is a golden
page of Anglican history. " The rest of her life was

less a series of events than a development of its inner spirit and its outward activities." She died on the Feast of St. Luke, October 18, 1923. But more must be said of Mackonochie.

Broken by litigation, driven from St. Alban's, he took a holiday with the Bishop of Argyll. One day a telegram arrived. It ran: "Our dear Brother Mackonochie has been taken to his rest." Mother Kate writes:

> The surroundings of his last moments are grand beyond measure. He who had lived his whole life, spending and being spent in the service of God and His Church amidst the throng and battle of mankind, in the din of the crowded city, gave up his spirit on the lonely mountain side, surrounded by the everlasting hills, alone with Him Whom he had loved and served all the days of his life.

He had set out on a long walk on the morning of December 15, 1887, accompanied by the Bishop's dogs. He was overtaken by a violent storm, and in the darkness could not fight against the howling wind, and lay down in the snow.

> The night came, and he never returned, and the Bishop and several parties of gillies and shepherds sought for two nights and two days unsuccessfully; and on the Saturday evening, despairing and sick of heart, were about to abandon the search as unsuccessful, when one of the men, glancing up the hill-side, saw the silhouette of the deer-hound sitting bolt upright against the snowy background, and immediately sent to tell the Bishop, who was with another party of searchers. When he arrived, he found the whole band of keepers and shepherds drawn

in a semi-circle in a snowy hollow, kept at bay by the
two dogs, who refused to let a creature approach, till
they caught sight of their master, when they sprang forward with a cry of joy. . . . There, in a snow wreath
. . . lay the weary body of Christ's faithful soldier and
servant, his head pillowed on his hands, and a pall of
spotless snow veiling the features. . . . As the Bishop
knelt to detach the head from the snow wreath in which
it lay, the dark clouds broke behind the mountains of
Glencoe, and the whole west was flooded with a glorious
golden light. . . .

One would hesitate, in charity, to say that the
Church Association was responsible for Mackonochie's
death, but I believe that it broke him mentally and
physically. Of him it may be said, and it suffices :

> We were weary, and are
> Fearful, and are in our march
> Fain to drop down and die.
> Still thou turnedst, and still
> Beckonedst the trembler, and still
> Gavest the weary thy hand !
> If in the paths of this world,
> Stones might have wounded thy feet,
> Toil or dejection have tried
> Thy spirit, of that we saw
> Nothing ! To us thou wert still
> Cheerful and helpful and firm.
> Therefore to thee it was given
> Many to save with thyself ;
> And at the end of the day,
> O faithful Shepherd ! to come,
> Bringing thy sheep in thy hand.

A. M. D. G.

INDEX

INDEX

INDEX

INDEX

INDEX

Trinity College, Oxford, 22, 62, 183, 196
Turner, Professor C. H., 197
Twelve Good Men, 91

Uganda, Bishop of, 189, 191
University Church of St. Mary's, 24, 25, 26, 65, 100
Ussher, 28

Vatican Council, 117
Vernon, Father, 17
Victoria, Queen, 149, 199

Waggett, Father, 18
Wagner, Arthur, 16
Wainwright, Father, 18, 42
Warburton, R. E., 219
Ward, Wilfred, 15, 23, 33
Water Babies, The, 31

Watson, Sir Wm., 127
We do See Life, 205
Wesley, John, 12, 69, 223
Westcott, Bishop, 72, 163
Westerton, Mr., 129
Weston, Dr. Frank, 18, 189–197
Whately, 65
Wilberforce, Robert, 51, 63
Wilberforce, Samuel, 113, 154
Williams, Dr. N. P., 18
Williams, Isaac, 51, 52, 54, 57, 60–8
Woodside, Croydon, 203
Wordsworth, 72, 90, 100
Wordsworth, Charles, 111
Wordsworth, Christopher, 111
Wynter, Dr. 82

Yonge, Charlotte Mary, 73, 217